THE GAME INVENTOR'S HANDBOOK

2ND EDITION

THE GAME
INVENTOR'S
HANDBOOK

2ND EDITION

Steve Peek

BETTERWAY BOOKS
CINCINNATI, OHIO

Typography by Park Lane Production Services

97 96 95 94 93   5 4 3 2 1

Library of Congress Cataloging-in-Publication Data

Peek, Stephen
    [Gameplan]
    The game inventor's handbook / by Steve Peek. -- 2nd ed.
       p.   cm.
    Includes index.
    ISBN 1-55870-315-2
    1. Games--Marketing. I. Title.
HD9993.G352P44   1993
794'.068--dc20   93-4791
                                                     CIP

Contents

A Word About Card Games
Making Computer Games

PART 6: MARKETING

Market Dynamics
Product Life Cycles
Market Tiers Defined
Marketing: What Is It?
Planning
Pricing
Consumer Advertising
The Circuit—Get Out and Sell
In-Store Demonstrations
Independent Stores

Buying Exposure
Working for Exposure
Having Exposure Thrust on You
Press Releases
Press Agents & Public Relations Firms
Product Tie-Ins

Traditional Toy & Game Market
Educational Market
Book Market
Gift and Stationery Market
Specialty Market
The Psychology of Buying
The Sub-Markets

Copyrights, Patents and Trademarks
Trade Shows and Conventions
Trade Associations
Glossary of Terms

Introduction

I have a story to tell. It goes like this...

In the year 1454, in the town of Mainz, Germany, Johann Gutenberg had just finished binding his first Bible. Ecstatic, he sought an audience with the local baron, from whom he sought financial assistance. With tremendous pride, he delivered the fruits of his lifetime of labor into the hands of this elegantly dressed nobleman. The baron opened the book and casually thumbed through its beautifully printed pages. He closed it, placed it on the desk and, with his right index finger, thoughtfully tapped the massive volume. "Herr Gutenberg, this is marvelous! Truly a wonder!," he exclaimed. "But, you see, I have this idea for a game and..."

The rest, as they say, is history. I'm sure the baron convinced poor, trusting Johann to go into partnership on a board game venture. And I'm pretty sure they went to work immediately printing the baron's new game, whatever it was, because the next year Mr. Gutenberg went bust and was forced to sell his press. He should have stuck with Bibles.

This isn't exactly a cheery note on which to start a book about getting into the game business. The painful truth is that out of an estimated three thousand games that enter the market every year, barely a handful will be found on retailers' shelves two years later. The rest are destined to gather dust in warehouses, basements and garages. In some cases, the games won't even remain on the market long enough to have a chance at becoming moneymakers.

GAME MARKETING

Marketing games is very different from selling books or movies—almost opposite, in fact. When a new book or movie is released by a major publisher, it is launched with a great deal of publicity and promotion. Advertising space is bought in newspapers, magazines, on radio and television. Six to eight weeks later the publisher or film producer not only knows whether it's a winner: he also can gauge how big a winner it will be and act accordingly. This pattern does not hold true for games.

WORD OF MOUTH IS THE KEY

The fact is, virtually every game that became a blockbuster was on the market for at least three years before anybody knew it was a hit. The reason: a game's popularity builds momentum, or loses it, by word-of-mouth. Someone plays a game at a friend's place. If she likes it, she buys it to play with someone else; and so forth. It's slow work, but if the product is a good one, it is the only kind of "advertising" that produces lasting results.

Several major companies have tried to shorten this tedious process by spending huge amounts of money promoting games. Sometimes it works, but more often than not it doesn't. One company spent nearly $10 million advertising a new game in its first year. The advertising bought a lot of shelf space in stores (more about this later), but the game grossed less than $8 million. This game is still on the market today, but it is not one people talk about.

This all sounds rather negative ... because it is. If you are serious about getting a game into print, however, you should be aware of the pitfalls before you start. Many people tend to look past these details and concentrate only on visions of wealth, fame, and glory. An important first step is to understand one's motivations, to determine exactly why you want to create games.

Game companies—those engaged in the design, manufacture and distribution of games—do it to make money. Most individuals who invent games think they also are doing it for the money, but this is not always the case. The real reason is ego: everybody wants a chance to be a big fish in the game pond. By publishing a game you join a small, elite group of people who have overcome anxieties about personal failure and financial loss and thrown caution to the winds in an effort to fulfill a dream. How many will make it big?

After nearly twenty years in the game business I have met, corresponded with, spoken to, or heard from thousands of people who invented a game they wanted to publish. Of these, I can think of at least eight who became wealthy as a result of their efforts. A number of others have achieved some success and made some money, but—as far as I know—only these eight really scored.

Since I am a medium-sized fish in the gaming pond, I am visited by a steady stream of people seeking advice on how to get published. It's a little like being a doctor. As soon as someone discovers your profession they begin talking about their pains—in my case, their games. It seems nearly everyone I meet believes he has at least one good game inside him. In most cases, unfortunately, that's the best place for it.

These individuals believe *if they could only get the game published* they would make a fortune. Many of these starry eyed inventors drift away in the middle of my negative lecture. Only a few diehards remain, stubbornly insisting they are going to get their games into print. Sometimes I help them; and sometimes I don't.

DETERMINATION IS ESSENTIAL—BUT NO GUARANTEE

In 1980, a recently widowed lady in her late sixties came to me. She and her husband had bred dogs all their lives and she had devised a game based on dog shows. She was prepared to spend nearly all her meager inheritance, money she would need later in life for a decent retirement. I thought breeders and other dog show devotees might find the game somewhat interesting, even though it struck me as being a bit dull. The biggest problem, I felt, was that the game would have such a limited market there was little chance it would be profitable. Therefore, I tried to convince the lady not to do it at all. Failing this, I hoped to talk her into making an extremely limited test run of a thousand copies. While her unit cost per unit would be very high, it would be a way she could test the product without gambling away her future security.

She refused to listen. She insisted on having 10,000 copies finished and delivered within three months. I told her I didn't think she should do the game and that, in good conscience, I could not produce it for her. When she said she would find someone else I recommended some printers and converters I knew to be honest and wished her luck. Twelve years later, as far as I know, she still had eight thousand games stuffing her garage and two bedrooms of her home.

The point of this story is not to be negative, but to stress that if you are serious about doing a game, you absolutely must share a trait with the lady dog breeder—determination. (Of course, doing a little test marketing before "taking the plunge" is not a bad idea either.) If you don't have determination, you had better forget the whole thing. You will just be wasting time and money.

Okay. Let's assume you are serious and determined to let nothing stand in your way. First, permit yourself to run through this little test. Be honest in answering now!

THE PROSPECTIVE GAME CREATOR'S NO-WIN QUIZ

1. Suppose no game publisher will buy your game and you are forced to publish it yourself. Regardless of how efficient you are about reducing costs, your game is going to cost somewhere around $30,000 for a limited test run. Can you afford to lose this much money?

2. Are you prepared to work for a minimum of three years at marketing the game, incurring substantial additional expense, to determine if it will become a success?

3. Are you willing to work nights and weekends, in addition to your regular full-time employment, filling orders, invoicing, maintaining books, creating advertisements, and attending trade and consumer shows? Are you willing to do all of this—and more—in addition to lying awake at night worrying about your investment?

4. Are you willing to do all these things, knowing the odds are heavily against you and that at best you may break even?

5. Are you willing to endure all this just for a chance to make a big splash in what is really a pretty small pond?

If you answered NO to any of these questions, you will be better off trying something else. If you are unsure about taking a gamble on your game, my advice is to go to Las Vegas. Plunk down ten thousand dollars on a roulette number and take your chances. Not only will the end come a lot more quickly and be less painful, the odds of your winning are better.

However, if you answered YES to all the questions, bless your heart: it looks as though you are ready to dive into the risk-filled waters of the gaming pond. Get ready for the time of your life! All forewarnings aside, it just may be the most rewarding adventure you will ever have.

ON YOUR MARK, GET SET, GO!

Once you make the decision to go ahead with your game, you should know that the odds are against your selling it to an existing game company. While this book will tell how to go about approaching game publishers, the author assumes you are so bull-headed and stubborn you are determined to get this game published no matter what—even if it means having to pay to do it yourself.

PART 1: History of Games

CHESS INVENTED 4000 YEARS AGO

The history of games is tied to Man in the same way Man's history is connected to conflict. It's interesting to know that *Hounds and Jackals*, the game beautiful, young Nefertiti and wise old Rameses played in the movie, *The Ten Commandments*, was a real game. It is fascinating to play chess and to learn about its origins. Some believe chess actually was invented in China around 2,000 B.C., not during the European Dark Ages as was commonly believed.

It is intriguing to read about artifacts from civilizations long gone (predating written history) that clearly demonstrate the existence of games in the most primitive societies. And, in the "nothing ever changes" department, to discover that Roman soldiers, faced with the tedium of duty in foreign lands, shot an ancient form of *Craps* for the robe of Jesus.

All this is interesting to a point, but if the book continued in this vein it would cease to be interesting and become just a parade of facts, names, and dates. Fortunately (for those bored by history), much of gaming's past does in fact pre-date written history and is subject to much speculation. For example there are at least seven versions recounting the origin of *Go*, Japan's national game, and even more stories about the invention of chess. What may be fascinating is a comparison of the development of games along with the social evolution of Man.

WAR: A THEME OF GAMES FOR CENTURIES

In the beginning it's almost certain games were primarily physical. Who could throw the farthest and straightest, run the fastest, hit the hardest; games intuitively designed to improve survival odds. Then, when man discovered leisure time, at some point during the Neolithic era, games began to assume the characteristics of man's greatest endeavor—war; organized running and hitting, still designed to improve an individual's chance of survival. Chess certainly has its roots in warfare, as do Checkers and *Go*.

War remained the dominant theme in games for many centuries and naturally so. War, even into our own era, remains the greatest undertaking of mankind. The connection between war and gaming is so close that in Prussia in 1811, during one of those rare momentary respites when politicians were not challenging each other over national property lines, Baron von Reisswitz and his son took the abstract pieces off the chess board and replaced them with cannon, infantry, and cavalry, turning an intellectual pastime into a training tool designed to increase the survival odds.

But war is only one path. Man has other conflicts in his checkered history and games seem naturally to follow conflict. Sometime during the Middle Ages there was an invention that changed life and civilization profoundly. Before this invention, wealth could be measured only in precious metals, jewels, land, slaves, and other real assets. Most of the real assets were held by nobility, who unleashed legions of headbashers to collect most of precious metals common people had obtained by selling potatoes and other foodstuffs.

The wealth was pretty much controlled by nobility and one was either born to that status or not. Consequently, very little creativity was devoted to developing wealth. There was only so much of it and the nobility had virtually all of it. If a nobleman wanted to increase his share, he had only to unleash more headbashers than the lord in the neighboring castle and take his wealth. Since a trained headbasher cost almost as much as a decent horse, nobles tended not to risk them against opposing headbashers very often.

Things stayed pretty much the same until two things happened; the invention of paper money and the ability to put this paper representation of real assets into financial institutions where it could be recorded, traded, borrowed against, and loaned out at interest ... even impounded by irate noblemen who sensed their wealth/power base was eroding. It takes more than the threat of headbashing to stop a great idea. Financial institutions flourished, creating the next conflict for gaming —the concept of getting rich.

THE HUNT FOR WEALTH— A GREAT GAME

Nothing has spawned more games than the hunt for wealth. Real estate, stock market, gambling, business—and even educational games —use as their central appeal the prospect of accumulating vast amounts of money. When it comes to getting rich, nothing is sacred. There are games dealing with selling dope, getting into heaven; even entering politics and wars for profit.

MORE COMPLEX GAMES REFLECT SOCIAL CHANGE

Just as man has become more sophisticated, so have games. What was once a black and white, good versus evil world is now a world filled with countless shades of gray. Gaming, being an integral part of humanity, has followed suit, changing once simple abstract rules into complex collections of often redundant verbiage intended to simulate incredibly intricate social patterns and events.

Where will it end? No one knows, not with any confidence anyway. Every year there are those who gamble their real wealth on an idea for a game which they are sure will catch the fancy of the current generation and turn them, the game entrepreneurs, into 20th century nobility.

But one thing is certain. Although there is some prosperity derived from fad games, the games which feed on our most basic conflicts and desires are the ones which become the phenomenal successes, the ones apt to last as long as chess and the other classics.

What will they be like, these super successes? Perhaps a survey of the games since World War II will provide a glimpse of what is to come.

GAMES IN THE TWENTIETH CENTURY

Like all other consumer products, games are born of societal conditions. By examining society we can understand the games emerging from it.

The 50s

Bobby socks and Hula Hoops, the birth of rock and roll, and the beginning of the space race. The Eisenhower Years were a time of tranquillity and prosperity. Everything made by Mitsubishi had recently been shot down over the Pacific. The Federal deficit went from 6.1 billion surplus in 1951 to a negative 12.9 billion in 1959. A man named Ray Kroc became involved with a hamburger stand called McDonald's and Coca Cola paid farmers one hundred dollars to allow their famous red and white logo to be painted on barn roofs.

But the big change was television. Initially a curiosity, it was to become an almost addictive way of life. It prompted the president of Boston University to ask, "Will television create a nation of morons?" There were some board games born to the fifties—*Yahtzee*, *Chutes & Ladders* and *CANDY LAND*—but the really big games, the ones people were talking about and the ones with which they were engrossed, were games like *Truth or Consequences*, *You Bet Your Life*, *I've Got a Secret*, *GE College Bowl*, and *What's My Line*. T.V. proved people would rather look at almost anything than at each other.

The 60s

If the fifties were tranquil, the sixties were times of conflict. The number of "advisors" in Viet Nam rose to over 500,000. Flower children preached free love and the dream of a black minister in Atlanta brought about social upheaval. The concrete clover leaf became our national flower. The federal deficit went to 25.2 billion and the television news media emerged as one of the world's most powerful forces.

Many games of the 60s reflected conflict. *Stratego*, *Risk* and the emergence of Avalon Hill, a game company with a whole line of pure military games. These games were opposed to gentler products of the same period; games like *The Game of Life* and *Careers*, games which reflected traditional values of family, country, religion. Game companies flourished and grew in what was for them a stable period.

The 70s

The 70s—the age of enlightened liberalism, protest marches, and the silent majority. Richard Nixon told us, "I am not a crook," but the implications of Watergate caused us to lose faith in our leadership. After serving billions of burgers, Ray Kroc up and McDied on us. Sony invaded the U.S. with VCR's. Jimmy Carter got elected president because he told us he would never lie. Throughout my entire life, people said anyone in America could be elected president. Nixon and Carter proved it. Oh yes, the federal deficit climbed to 79.4 billion.

The games of the 70s were a little card game called *UNO*, which this year will pass the one hundred million mark in units sold, and an incredibly strange game, without a board, called *DUNGEONS & DRAGONS*, which launched a whole new category of products.

The 80s Moving into the 80s we found hostages and terrorism and a proliferation of computers at work and at home. People paid up to fifty dollars for sweat shirts with that red and white Coca Cola logo on it. By the end of the decade the hardest thing to find in Russia was a Stalinist and the national debt passed two trillion dollars. The 80s produced two megahits in the game business — *Trivial Pursuit* and *PICTIONARY*. Both exploited the ground broken by *DUNGEONS & DRAGONS* in taking the focus of a social interactive game away from the board and putting it in the environment with the players.

The 90s What will the 90s bring, socially and game-wise? No one can say for certain but a few clues might be gleaned by looking at some current trends. Do you remember the work place before computer work stations began to dominate the office landscape? Open bays, typewriters clicking, and people arguing about sports and politics by the water cooler. Lots of personal interaction. Maybe you couldn't hear yourself think but there were constant exchanges of ideas and information.

The work place today is a maze of unconnected cubicles. Cut off from humanity we sit eyes glued to computer screens with micro headsets plugged into our ears. We are starved for social interaction. *DUNGEONS & DRAGONS*, *Trivial Pursuit*, and *PICTIONARY* are all social interactive games. People want contact with other people. After a day of isolation with high-tech equipment, we want a "high-touch" environment at home. Games which are socially interactive, of low competitiveness and that encourage team play are likely to remain popular well into and through the 90s.

Another factor affecting the development of games in the coming years is the perceived dismal state of the U.S. system of public education. Concerned parents will take a more active role in their children's education at home. Games that both amuse and educate should rise in popularity.

And finally, consider the rise to increasing affluence of the baby boomers. Our parents were children of the Great Depression. Hard lessons taught them not to waste, to make do with what they had, and to buy practical things of value. Our parents tried to instill the same values in us but their efforts were offset by television, billboards and radio ads pitching the good life.

There was recently an ad in the newspaper for a Mercedes for $75,000. On the facing page there was an ad for a $15,000 Ford. The line drawings looked remarkably similar. Seen together the ads prompt the question: is a Mercedes five times better than a Ford? The answer, objectively a no, subjectively maybe a yes. People buy a Mercedes not because it is five times better than a Ford but because they want it and can afford it.

Clever Endeavor was a game that experienced a meteoric launch in 1989. It retailed for $35.00. I thought the price was too high, but it had extras: gold ink, elegantly made custom plastic playing pieces, and a velvet bag. All of these things added perceived value. *Trivial Pursuit*, which originally sold for $40.00, possessed the same kind of perceived value. What's the lesson? Simple. In the 90s you can sell your products for more if they possess perceived value, the extras that surprise and please the customer when they get the product home.

The 90s will be a time for aggressive entrepreneurs. *Trivial Pursuit, PICTIONARY, UNO, DUNGEONS & DRAGONS, Pente,* and *MONO-POLY* have something in common. Not one of these blockbusters originated within a major game company. They all came from entrepreneurs.

In the 90s we will face many problems. We are going to have increased foreign competition. We will experience a rise in raw material costs. But history shows us, at least in the game industry, that victory more often comes from David's sling than from Goliath's sword. The coming decade can be an exciting time for those who look the challenge in the eye ... for those who aren't content to do things the same old way ... for those who are willing to expand and diversify ... for those who refuse to surrender.

If you don't get a hit the first time, sling another stone. You might bring down that next giant.

PART 2: Inventing Games

You may already have invented a game. At the very least, you probably have one in mind. Nonetheless, **don't** skip this section unless you are not interested in improving your game concept or in inventing others. This chapter outlines the steps in the inventing process. While its focus is specifically and totally on inventing games, the process itself is valid for inventing almost anything.

IDEAS: GENERATION AND VIABILITY

Charlie Phillips is one of my dearest friends and a prolific game inventor. He has sold twelve ideas to half a dozen major companies in the last ten years and is the most consistently creative idea man I know. Twenty years ago he worked in what is called an idea factory. He was paid eight dollars an hour to sit at a drawing board eight hours a day. The boss would come in, go to a blackboard and write down a topic; automobile door handles or bicycle handlebar grips, for example.

The room full of aspiring (and perspiring, to hear Charlie tell it) inventors hunched over their tables and madly sketched idea after idea about whatever the subject of the moment happened to be. After a while the boss returned, collected everyone's sketches, posted another theme and retired to his office to peruse the stack of inventions. Each employee was expected to generate a minimum of **sixty** ideas a day. The company owned all rights to them. If an idea was sold and manufactured, the inventor was more likely to find out about it while walking through a store than from the idea factory where the concept was created.

While this was a high pressure, thankless job, one which sucks creativity from individuals and then casts them aside, it was a powerful training field. Charlie escaped long before the process burned him out. In fact, it is hard to imagine Charlie ever running out of ideas. He has them by the bunches. He can not fill his automobile gas tank without coming up with four or five. Each morning's shower usually produces an even dozen. The guy drives everyone around him crazy with his constant outpouring of ideas.

Obviously, they are not all gems. Most of them only serve as part of the brainstorming process; i.e., the idea is not to evaluate while you are creating. Charlie's theory might be summed up with a formula which creates a ratio of volume quantity of ideas of uneven quality to a small number of ideas that have real merit. How does Charlie do it? How does one man get so many ideas?

In Charlie's case, as with a number of inventors, it is a combination of stream of consciousness thinking, a unique perspective, and persistent childlike curiosity. Stream of consciousness might work like this.

Stream of Consciousness

Stream of consciousness is simply letting your mind slide from one thought or image to another, unhampered by mental criticism. In contemporary jargon it is switching off the left side of the brain and turning up the power to the right side. Even if you aren't the least interested in inventing it can be a fun and entertaining experience.

Unique Perspective

Unique perspective is simple to demonstrate. Look where the floor meets the wall. Imagine a cartoon mouse sticking its head from the hole, nervously twitching whiskers as its gleaming eyes watch you. Now, close your eyes and become the mouse. Imagine what it sees. Is there furniture in the room? Does it loom like fabric covered cliffs? Does the carpet piling come up to its shoulders? What does it think of you? How does it react when you rise from the chair?

While this can be an endless game and may not seem to serve much purpose it is the most simple form of a problem solving technique.

For example, you just invented this great game where each player has a popgun and a number of pingpong balls. In the center of the table a miniature basketball net and backboard spins around. Each player fires the pingpong balls trying to trap them in the net. First player to sink all his balls wins. Great game, but a trip down to Toys-R-Us reveals there already is something very similar on the market—too similar to make your idea interesting to a manufacturer.

Back to the Drawing Board

Here's where changing perspective comes in. You run home and start a new model. This time the center of the table contains a self-loading baseball "pitcher's arm" that spins around, catapulting colored pingpong balls randomly. The players are armed with huge, floppy foam catcher's mitts, and the first player to catch five balls wins. Maybe the ball reservoir is filled with toy "slime" and you call the game *SPIT BALL*! By simply changing perspective we have a new game that looks to be even better than the original. Always, *always* run ideas through this process.

Childlike Curiosity

Of all our personality traits, childlike curiosity is the easiest to explain but probably the hardest to maintain as we age. When children have a basic understanding of speech but little knowledge of how anything works every parent will tell you they drive people crazy with two words, "what" and "why."

If you apply this simple technique to each idea you can only enrich the concept. An example would be watching a child playing with blocks. You ask yourself why the child likes doing it. Your answer is they like to build things. Then you begin a series of "what if's." What if the blocks were plastic? What if they were different shapes but still fit together? What if each block contained snapping sockets so they would not fall down. Bingo!

Viability

Once you have the idea, it must be tested for viability. Lacking a history of industry products and a two-ton file of game company catalogs you are forced to investigate the originality of the idea by visiting toy stores. After haunting their aisles and talking to store managers who have excellent memories you may find out the game has been manufactured and failed in so many previous versions that it is not worth doing.

A good example of this is a game based on *Liar's Poker*. Most people know *Liar's Poker* as a bar game played on pay days. Each player bids from a dollar bill using the serial numbers on his bill plus the numbers he suspects are on his opponent's bill. Each bid must be higher than the last. (i.e. two 5s beats two 4s; three 4s beats two 5s). This continues until one player believes the other player has overbid and calls. The winner gets to keep both bills. Simple, fun and it has been popular for years. So popular in fact that about every other year some unsuspecting entrepreneur manufactures a garage full, then runs into a stone wall trying to sell them.

When a game fails that often there is something fundamentally wrong with the concept. In the case of *Liar's Poker* the problem is players really want to gamble. They don't enjoy playing with play money. When you run into this situation, no matter how good you feel your idea is, put it aside and start on something more productive.

GAME CATEGORIES

Another test for concept viability is market niche or category. Product category makes a world of difference as to which company, if any, might be interested in an idea. Some categories have higher interest levels than others and some hold no interest at all for certain manufacturers. Some categories are broad with new products added to them each year. Others have little turnover, remaining as staples for the companies that own them.

Learn what categories mean to a company, and keep abreast of changes in the industry. Trends and other product successes can cause a company to change its policies in a second if they see potential for significant profit.

Current categories rated by general interest levels among major game manufacturers are as follows. Bear in mind these can change as quickly as the weather.

Game Categories of No Interest

Educational
Religious
Checkers/Chess variants
Two player abstract strategy

Stock market/Business
Sports based board games
Gambling based board games

Game Categories of Low Interest

Pre-school (*Memory*) games
Family (*Clue*)
Card (*Racko*)
Travel (*Connect Four*)
Three dimensional strategy (*Battleship*)
Adventure (*Hero Quest*)
Word (*SCRABBLE*)

Game Categories of Fair Interest

Electronic table (*Simon*)
Electronic hand held (*Gameboy*)

Game Categories of High Interest

Pre-school Plastic Action (*Crocodile Dentist*)
Jr. Plastic Action (*Shark Attack*)
Skill & Action (*Perfection*)
Girl's (*Girl Talk*)
Adult Social Interactive (*SCATTERGORIES*)

THEME

The third step after checking concept viability and category fit is make sure the theme has a home with a game manufacturer.

Novice inventors almost always resist changing a game's theme at first. Many don't believe it can be done successfully. They are wrong on both counts.

The theme is often used as part of the hook in packaging and promoting the product. If the theme does not possess mass market appeal game company acquisition people are going to yawn and say, "pass ... next item" about one minute into your presentation.

Trendy themes (movies, songs, current events), like games themselves, come from societal conditions and changes. What is popular this year probably will be out of style two years from now.

Sometimes Timing Is Everything

The trick is to tie your game into a theme that is on the rise, not one that is cresting. A good example of this is what happened at the start of the Persian Gulf War. When Operation Desert Shield began sending troops to Saudi Arabia one company got lucky. They were about to release a game about a war in the Middle East. When they saw what was happening they added United Nations military forces to their unreleased game and had it on the market in thirty days. It received tons of free publicity and sold like hot cakes—for a while.

The other side of the same coin showed itself when a number of companies brought out similar products, but only after Desert Shield became Desert Storm. Savvy retailers saw the end of the marketing potential for Desert Storm products and simply refused to buy enough quantity to make the late games viable. It turned out they were right. A month after Desert Storm was over you couldn't give product away.

A more positive example is about an inventor who was interested in airlines. He created an airline theme card game with some very interesting mechanics and game play. The idea was each player represented an airline company. By playing sets of cards he could establish routes and score points or hamper other players. The player with the most routes won the game.

The way the game play worked is what made the game interesting. The fact it was about airline companies had nothing to do with it. When the inventor finally was convinced no one was interested in a game about the airline industry he took a suggestion to re-theme the game. When you see someone playing a card game about dinosaur herds, remember it started out as a game about airlines.

Re-theming Your Game

The bottom line is this. You should constantly be thinking and rethinking of ways to re-theme a game. Never be satisfied until you have signed a contract and deposited the royalty advance check. And always, always, *always* be open to suggestions from game companies. When you are showing a company a game about becoming a movie star and they say, "I love the idea but movie games are out. Can you make it about *Slime Kittens from the Nth Dimension*?", your response should be, "Is tomorrow morning too late?"

GAMEPLAY: MECHANICS AND DEVICES

You should be starting to understand that all of this works together. A viable concept fits a product category, the category supports the theme, and all of that creates an environment for what is called gameplay.

Gameplay is the seldom mentioned aspect of games that make them fun. Without good gameplay, all the other elements are so much window dressing. But like everything else gameplay has to be more than good. It has to fit the product environment.

Just as an engineer would never try to fit a 747 turbo jet engine to a Honda, a game inventor has to make sure the way the game plays and the devices used in it are appropriate to the theme and category. It would be a terrible blunder to design a game using small beads for a preschool game. The kids will either lose or eat the beads.

Spinners are good for kid games because they can't lose them. Adults think spinners are juvenile and prefer dice. Kids often don't understand the concept of time and consequently don't use timing devices included in a game. Adults get impatient when one player takes too long with a turn. So they like timers.

When questioning whether gameplay or devices fit a certain category it's a good idea to invest a little money in building your game library. Go buy a half dozen games currently selling in the same category and study them. See what they have in common. Also look to see if any of them incorporate your planned devices or mechanics.

PROTOTYPES

Once you have found a publisher who has agreed to examine your game, make sure it goes out ready to play. Never, under any circumstances, send a game out until the publisher has agreed to accept it. Don't ever send in a prototype with a note instructing the prospective party to find his own game money or just to use checkers for the men. Game publishers want something they can pass directly on to their playtesters. They don't look at the product again until the initial playtest reports have been presented.

It's also a good idea to send the prototype in a box rather than an envelope, making certain all the playing pieces are separated and secured to keep them from getting jumbled in the mail. Consider the following a helpful rule of thumb: the better a first impression the prototype makes, the better its chances are of being given serious consideration. That applies all the way up the line—from playtesting to marketing.

PLAY VALUE—THE ESSENTIAL INGREDIENT

Several years ago something happened to me that proves that last point. I received a unique inquiry from a designer wanting to submit a game. Rather than send a letter, the enterprising fellow sent a short one-act play purportedly set in my office, consisting of a dialogue between the designer and myself. The approach was so clever I felt I had to give the fellow a chance. I wrote back saying we would examine the game—but, no promises.

My jaw dropped when the prototype arrived on my desk. It was nothing short of beautiful. At first I thought it already had been printed, but close examination revealed it to be an exceedingly clever and professional job by an expert graphic artist. The game really scored high with me because it made me aware the inventor cared enough to spend the money to show it in such an excellent light.

After examining all the attractive and high quality components, I looked at the rules. Seeing that they were well-written and noting that the subject matter held marketing possibilities, I sent it on to the playtesters.

When the report came back my jaw dropped again. The playtesters had accomplished something very rare for a game company: they found the game to have no play value whatsoever. Dumbfounded, I sent it out again, this time to a different set of playtesters. The report came back the same.

Sad ending notwithstanding, the point is that the prototype was so well made and so enticing I was induced to spend my time and that of two groups of playtesters on a game that otherwise would have been sent back the same day it arrived.

The quality of the presentation earned it serious consideration but ultimately the game's complete lack of play value doomed it.

PHYSICAL DESIGN: ORIGINAL AND FINAL PROTOTYPES

If there are two hundred professional game inventors, there probably are that many opinions on prototyping. Some inventors have such strong reputations and relationships with game companies their first prototype may be no more than a pencil sketch. Others lean toward the opposite end of the spectrum. Using high powered computers, graphics software, workshops and model makers every prototype they turn out is an expensive, near perfect rendition of the final product. Most inventors have neither the established relationships to submit a drawing on a bar napkin nor the reservoir of capital to support perfect prototypes at every level. The vast majority of inventors work somewhere between the two extremes.

The system that works for me and others I know is a three tiered system.

Original Prototype This can be a very crude model. Its only purpose is to prove the concept to the inventor's initial satisfaction. It can be no more than a large sheet of paper decorated and ruled with color markers.

Testing Prototype Usually one of these is not enough, so be prepared to make as many as are necessary to finish the playtesting successfully. This stage prototype does not need to be perfect but it does need to be attractive, pleasing, and professional. It is going to be used to debug the concept, the game mechanics, and the written rules. People you find to test your game are only human, which is why you want them testing in the first place. They will form first impressions based on what they see when you put the game in front of them, so it is important not to have them entertaining negative thoughts about your game before they even play it.

Most games develop problems that can be solved only by changing the prototype. Do not be disappointed if halfway through the first playtest session someone says, "Hey, this is dumb. The marble hole needs to be on the corners where I can reach it and the discard pile should be in the middle where everyone can see it." If that happens, it's good news; the testers are doing their job. If the testers come up with valid complaints, make the changes before the next test session. It will take time and cost money, but if you are not prepared to attend to valid complaints from your playtesters, why test.

A typical game goes through four to six prototypes at this level. I was involved with one game that went through two dozen changes and never was right.

Final Prototype This is the one you will be using to present the idea to game companies or to investors if you are planning to self publish. Don't skimp but don't go overboard either. Currently the best ways to make final prototypes involve complete, full color composite art or working with computer graphic programs. In either case you want to make sure that after the first one is complete you can make subsequent copies by using color photocopies or laser printer copies from your disk.

If you are self-publishing your game you may wish to go an extra step. Have the graphics person take the project through final production art. When that is approved, conduct one more series of tests to be absolutely certain there are no more changes. Then go to film. This is expensive but something you will have to do eventually before you can publish. Once the art is in film form you can have color proofs (match prints) made that will look as good as the final production run. These match prints can then be turned into a prototype game impressive enough to show anyone.

There is nothing more nerve-racking than placing the final prototype into a game testing session. You have expended all that time, energy and money to get this far. As a result of previous testing you already have made more changes than you ever dreamed possible and now you are terrified these new testers—individuals who have never seen your game—are going to find something so fundamentally wrong you will have to redo the whole thing.

This is a nightmare we all have. But if you have done your job with the previous tests (and if they have been fair and objective), and if you have been open-minded and genuinely sought testers' input you should be okay. Many an inventor, however, has discovered why valid test sessions are so important when it came time to pull out the check book to start all over on prototyping.

How Do You Build the #$@& Things?

Great. You know there are three levels of prototyping and you know the purpose of each, but . . . how do you actually make one?

Original prototypes for board games can be made by almost anyone. They can be crude as long as they are functional. If you don't feel competent to make yours, hand a crayon to a young school-age friend.

Creating board game testing prototypes requires some graphic skill. If you don't have it, can't develop it or borrow it from a friend or relative, you will have to buy it. That requires working with an artist. At this level you want an artist who works out of his or her home, has no overhead, and works for very little.

The final prototype requires professionalism. Once again, if you have some graphic skills you may be able to pull it off yourself. But don't be one of those myopic amateurs who doesn't realize how homemade his art really looks. If you can afford, or have access to, a good graphics computer and software learn how to use it. Computers, scanners, and software can go a long way toward making your efforts look professional.

Prototype Devices

Everything you have read to this point is valid for games' paper components; board, boxes, money, cards, rules, score pad, etc. But what about a game with a three-dimensional plastic catapult that launches fly-apart Slobovian knights against a castle wall that oozes slime?

I was afraid someone would ask that.

Unless you are an engineer or have one for a partner, and your device is mechanical with moving parts, you probably will have to hire a model maker. Take a deep breath. If you thought graphic artists were expensive, get ready for a shock. Most of these guys are very good at what they do, but what they do is exacting, takes a long time, and is a little more complicated than graphics. After all, graphics only have to look good. Models have to look good, function well, and hold up to repeated use.

If on, on the other hand, your project requires a three dimensional plastic, wood or metal part that isn't mechanical (i.e., does not have moving parts) you may be able, with a little extra effort, to make it yourself. If you are a model kit builder you already have most of the necessary skills to "scratch" build your prototype. If you are not a kit builder, or have never "scratch" built something, do a little creative research.

Make a trip to a few hobby shops and find out where the local models club meets. Go to a meeting and make friends with one or two modelers. Most are more than happy to share their knowledge. It will take a little while to find out exactly what types of plastics and adhesives or chemical bonders to use. Once you do, you should be able to get up to speed fairly quickly with a simple work table, some drafting equipment, and plastic materials.

Prototypes-R-Us

Not too long ago, a single copy of professional-looking graphics for prototypes could cost an inventor several thousand dollars. If a second copy was required less attractive color copies were used.

Things have changed. A lot of old graphic dogs have learned new tricks, using computers and ever-evolving new generations of software, scanners, and laser output devices. These new capabilities may still cost about the same as an original old style prototype, but three things are markedly different.

The inventor gets to see an excellent representation of the prototype's graphics before it is printed in final form. Making changes is inexpensive while you are proofing designs on a monitor. If the inventor anticipates needing more than one copy, not only are the second and subsequent copies relatively inexpensive, but unlike color copies they are the same quality as the original.

Many professional inventors are investing in their own computer and software systems. Their logic is that the money they save by not paying an independent graphic artist to design twenty or more prototypes a year will cover the cost of the equipment.

If you decide to take this approach, be careful. Just because you know how to run a sophisticated, high speed computer doesn't make you a good graphics designer. You still may want to hire out logo design, color selection, and layout, then scan it in yourself.

If you do hire outside artist be careful selecting your graphics person. There are many computer experts who have less graphic design talent than you have. It usually is best to find a great designer who has added a computer to augment his or her capabilities. These people tend to be less satisfied with the first level of computer graphics and constantly push the hardware and software to higher standards.

Probably the best test is to look at an artist's computer graphics portfolio. If it is obvious it all was done on a computer, find someone else.

Recently, a product acquisition chief was examining an excellent computer-generated prototype. He asked how long the game had been on the market. That kind of finished quality is available. It clearly has a dramatic impact and requires only that the inventor invest enough time to locate the right designer.

PLAYTESTING

When your intention is to sell to a publisher, creating a game is only a tenth of the battle. Your next step is the playtest, and it's a step you have to take before you even start to think about the submission process.

Games that appear to be a lot of fun in theory may crash completely when actually played. I recall investing a small fortune several years ago in an imported European game as a Christmas present for my son.

You probably will not be startled to learn I buy games the way other fathers buy train sets, and for substantially the same reason. I get to play too!

It Is More Expensive *not* to Playtest

This particular offering grabbed me at once. The box art was superb. The game was a science fiction board game and when the storekeeper let me take a peek inside, I saw that the box was full of gorgeous colorful pieces and cards. The whole package had a quality air and smelled like a real winner.

It wasn't. To this day the game has never been played in my house, either by its proud new owner or anyone else. This might have been the result of poor translation (the game originated in Spain) but I doubt it. The rules were clear enough, but putting them into practice was another matter. My guess is that despite the obvious talent and money that went into the finished package, somebody forgot about playtesting.

Playtesting lets you know where you have gone wrong in a game; where the weaknesses lie and, above all, where it lacks clarity. Clarity is critically important. When you develop a game, many of its aspects may be obvious to you, but not to someone who hasn't lived with the project for months. A good playtester will let you know where and how the game tripped him up. A good designer will take out all the flaws before submission.

Remember this. If a publisher is interested, the very first thing he's going to do is playtest. The effort invested in playtesting before submission will be worthwhile.

Three Levels of Playtesting

Like prototypes, I divide playtesting into three levels: original, debugging, final.

ORIGINAL TESTING

Original testing should be done first by the inventor or inventors, then by friends or family (friendly and supportive but typically unreliable). The inventor phase of the test may simply be the inventor sitting whole nights playing the game alone, trying to find loopholes in the rules or flaws in a three dimensional device. The object is simply to make sure each component in the game performs its function.

Next, waylay a few friends or relatives and tie them to kitchen chairs. Tell them their lives, as well as yours, hang in the balance and invite them to have fun. Don't put too much faith in how much they say they like the game. All you are looking for is proof the game's components work so you can proceed to the real testing.

DEBUGGING

Debugging, the second phase of testing, is hard on inventors. You want your product to be perfect and you believe it is perfect when you put it in front of strangers. But good testing results comes from strangers who have no vested interest in you, your product, or your feelings. It is difficult to remain objective and not become defensive when they start criticizing. Control yourself! Denying a problem is the worst possible position to take. Keep telling yourself this process is part of making your good game a great one.

FINAL PLAYTESTING

Final playtesting is subdivided into two stages: final and really final. In final testing you should be using the last of your second stage prototypes. If possible, have someone other than the game's inventor conduct the tests. In fact, it's better if the inventor is not even present. The testers should have to learn and play the game with the rules alone, unaided by verbal prompting. And, while I would do it as quietly as possible, set up a video recorder in some unobtrusive corner and let it run without an operator. You don't want the testers becoming self-conscious about being on camera.

These tests should be conducted and the game changed accordingly until the tests are perfect. The *really* final tests are conducted using the final prototype that will be used in the presentations. Really final playtests are dreaded by those inventors who, deep down inside, know they did not address all the comments from previous tests.

Where Do Playtesters Come From?

As mentioned earlier, Phase One playtesters include the inventor, his friends, and his family. Phase Two playtesters really should be strangers or, at worst, casual acquaintances.

One of my favorite resources for phase two playtesters is a playtest party. Ask a friend or neighbor to invite a specific number of people to your home on a Friday or Saturday night (daytime for children's games). Make sure the neighbor understands you prefer people you don't know. In fact, your neighbor's relatives will fill the bill nicely. When they show up, have plenty of refreshments, and maybe even some music. Create a genuine party atmosphere. Let everyone talk for a few minutes and get comfortable with one another. Remember that in real life people who share a game usually know each other.

When you feel the time is right, bring out the game. Judge their reactions from the time they look at the box to the time they help you clear the game off the table. This should be work for you but don't make it work for them. Keep the mood light and fun. Even though it might, don't act as if your future depends on the outcome. Encourage comments, suggestions, and criticisms. Always ask each tester, "What would you change to make it better?"

Other sources for Phase Two testers are church clubs or social organizations. (Catholic Women's League, singles clubs, senior clubs, etc.) These groups often look for interesting things to do as part of their monthly meetings.

If your game is a preschool product, your best bet is apt to be a day care center. Some will welcome your occupying an hour or so of some children's time, others may ask you to pay twenty-five to fifty dollars for the privilege. It's worth it.

Final and *really* final testing need to be conducted with genuinely objective groups. Some inventors, especially game companies, go so far as to pay marketing firms several thousand dollars to conduct what they call focus groups with people who answer ads in the newspapers, are screened for certain demographic qualities and are then paid to bring their children or play a game themselves.

The Perils of Playtesting

What could be perilous about playtesting? After all, you will hear it from everyone. Playtest, playtest, playtest ... you cannot do too much. But beware: the results obtained from playtesting are only as good as the way in which you conduct the tests. If you don't set up fair and impartial tests, you will be making an enormous mistake if you rely on the results of those tests.

The cost of relying on invalid information is obvious; from the waste of time and money, to bruised egos, to the embarrassment of a scathing rejection letter asking why you wasted the company's time submitting a flawed product. Here are six specific pitfalls to avoid when conducting playtest.

GIVING VERBAL INSTEAD OF WRITTEN INSTRUCTIONS

It is hard enough to find evaluators for a game without having to make them read rules. No one (at least not someone I would want at a playtest of mine) enjoys reading rules. But the way in which the rules are written is as important as the rules and the games themselves. You are not going to be standing beside players when they have a question about the game. You won't be able to answer any questions. If you don't evaluate your written rules ruthlessly, and identify which parts are unclear or confusing (even though you explained it in three different areas), your game will fail in the market or at the game company's test—even if it is great fun.

Also, if the rules are so long that no one wants to read them, your game (not just your rules) has a serious flaw. You can not separate the written rules from the game.

PLAY TESTING WITH FRIENDS OR RELATIVES

How many of you have friends or relatives who truly would feel comfortable telling you your baby is ugly? Not just ugly, but awkward and boring as well. Do you think you can really hide the fact that it is your baby; the baby you created and toiled over, the one which you are so proud of and for which you have such hopes? Will your friends or relatives feel they can be totally honest without hurting your feelings? *Then why would you ever rely on their opinions in a playtest?*

One answer is because you are proud of your creation and believe they will enjoy it, which negates the reason for conducting a playtest in the first place. Another common reason to justify using friends and relatives is they are more easily gathered to playtest a game than strangers.

Don't do what is easy, do what is reliable. Use your friends and relatives as very preliminary testers to see how the concept goes over. If they don't like the game and want to play every time they see you, go back to the drawing board. But once you get serious, find testers at day care centers, church groups, retirement homes, motor home camps, newspaper ads or whatever age/interest group fits your particular product.

The very last test should be conducted by someone other than yourself. No questions should be answered verbally and if possible make a homemade video tape of the event for you to evaluate later.

PROVIDING A "RECESS" FROM WORK, SCHOOL OR RESPONSIBILITY

As Larry Bernstein of Mattel said at the Game Inventors of America's 1992 Inventor Conference, "You can't take kids out of school, playtest a game, then ask them if they liked it. Compared to what they should have been doing, the game was a lot more fun. Digging for worms would be a lot more fun than school for many kids." For adult games set up your test sessions for after work, preferably at the same time the playtesters normally socialize.

COMMUNICATING YOUR HOPES FOR OR ATTACHMENT TO THE GAME

It is easy to cite obvious examples of this. Telling the playtesters they are testing your game. Phrasing questions with a positive spin such as "Isn't it fun?", and (don't laugh) telling playtesters how good the game is or why you think it will be successful. But there are more insidious ways of influencing playtesters that you should avoid, for example: defending any part of the game; getting excited if they get excited; handling or discussing your game with more care or pride than any other game that is being tested as a comparison. In short, your behavior and attitude toward your game can easily influence your playtesters' opinions, virtually guaranteeing invalid results.

COMPARING YOUR GAME TO THE WRONG BASE LINE

Game professionals never cease to be amazed by the number of comparisons of a new game to *MONOPOLY* or *Trivial Pursuit*. "The playtesters liked it better than *Trivial Pursuit*," read the neverending flow of letters pouring into product acquisition offices. The problem is consumers might not buy *MONOPOLY* or *Trivial Pursuit* if it were introduced today.

The game business is a fashion business; to a significant extent for new games, a fad business. Therefore, how your game compares to something that was introduced ten or fifty years ago is almost irrelevant. How does your game compare to things being valued by your target audience *today*? Things like Nintendo, VCR viewing, other new games or even hanging out in the mall. If your target audience won't give up another form of currently popular entertainment to play your game, how will your game succeed?

NOT HEARING WHAT YOU HEAR, NOT SEEING WHAT YOU SEE

It may be difficult to imagine how anyone could invest their time, money and effort in conducting a series of valid tests, then deny or try to explain away the results. But it happens all the time, and that anyone could be you. How? Because even though you will invest in conducting your playtests, you will have invested even more in the idea of your game succeeding. Everybody has dreams and aspirations, and for many of us, our game is the way we finally are going to realize our goals.

We *know* our game is different, unique. Success, money, and fame are just around the corner. Nothing will stop us, not even poor playtest results. In order to save yourself time, money and heartache, ask yourself before you begin each playtest if your game is going to succeed in the market. If your answer is anything other than "I don't know", or, after a lot of positive testing, "maybe," then postpone your test efforts until you are ready to hear the truth rather than what you want to hear.

PART 3: Selling a Game to a Publisher

Every inventor dreams that his or her game will become the next *Trivial Pursuit, Girl Talk, PICTIONARY, DUNGEONS & DRAGONS, UNO*, or *MONOPOLY*. Every dream cannot come true. Selling your game to a game publisher is desirable, but it is unlikely to be accomplished by the first-time game inventor.

PITCHING THE BIG LEAGUES

Let's face it. The dream of ultimate, big-time success is the siren's call that lures inventors into this very speculative industry. However, the odds against achieving this kind of success are incredibly high. Consider how many new games come out every year. Then consider that a phenomenon like *MONOPOLY* or *Trivial Pursuit* occurs maybe once every twenty years. Add to that scenario the difficulty of convincing a major company to even look at a new game from an unknown inventor and the whole ball game begins to look like a "no win" situation. It's very difficult ... but it's not impossible.

Before I started this book I mailed a letter of inquiry (under an assumed name) to the fifty largest board game companies in the United States. I already knew what they were going to say, but I wanted an official record. My letter stated at the start I did not have a game to show them. I explained that I was writing this book and that I would appreciate their sending me a statement of their official policy regarding outside submissions.

37 of the 50 companies did not bother to reply. The rest, with one exception, sent back a printed rejection letter, stating flatly that the firm would not examine or consider a game from an outside source under any circumstances. The one exception was a form letter with a hand written note scribbled on it inviting me to call, with the proviso that I would not mention the name of the individual or his firm in this book.

After speaking with this game world's "deep throat" I was able to confirm the following. Officially—on the record—his firm's policy was the same as all the others. In short, save your postage. Unofficially, as far as "deep throat" was aware, there are three ways to get a major company to even consider looking at an outsider's game.

UNDERSTANDING THE INDUSTRY

An inventor recently complained about the game industry. His visions of product acquisition heads playing musical chairs to funeral dirges produced cringes. His somber predictions of resignations, layoffs and early retirements generated images of depression era soup lines. Because corporate mergers and acquisitions make it more difficult for inventors, he tolled the industry's death knell.

While he had some valid points there is a reason for some of the shambles and confusion he describes—and it's not limited to the game industry. As most of us have noticed, society is experiencing one of history's great transitions. We are changing from a print-literate to an electronic-literate society. Whether this will be to mankind's ultimate benefit or lead to the demise of civilization "as we know it" is not the point. The point is this trend appears to be unstoppable.

After recognizing the transition to electronic literacy, the obvious question—at least in the context of this book—is: How does it affect inventors?

Here is a view from the game industry. The transition may well be unstoppable, but it is not fast. It has been going on for fifty years (if you don't count radio as the starting point). The "Golden Agers" (vigorously represented by AARP) will soon be the largest single population group in the country. They are the ones who still play games—and the ones who read. Bottom line: electronic wizardry will not completely replace board games for at least one and possibly two generations. Granted the board game market will continue to shrink, but it will be viable after I am buried.

The problem with many game companies is they are driven by quarterly profits. As the market erodes the bigger, publicly held, companies feel the weight of their overhead. Through mergers, acquisitions, layoffs, forced early retirements, and creative accounting they strive to maintain previous profit levels. The size of the game pond is evaporating. As the water disappears, the fish begin to eat one another so they can maintain their territory—their "market share". Pretty soon there are only a few fish—the winners—thrashing in the mud.

To make this specifically clear, examine the changes in major game companies in one year—1991. Milton Bradley acquired Parker Brothers, Western Publishing took over The Games Gang and Mattel Toys bought International Games. In one year the six largest game companies became the three largest game companies.

The prospect of the shrinking pond analogy would really be depressing if we could not add one ingredient to the analogy — crayfish. These little guys love mud and shallow water. Before the sun alerts buzzards with the first whiff of decay, they will be out of their holes busily carving up the big fish carcasses.

In the game industry, as in others, the crayfish are the little companies with their niche marketing strategies. As big companies get fewer and bigger, they leave vacuums. Smaller market categories that offer little nourishment to them provide banquets for the voracious crayfish.

Many inventors have spent their adult life in the game industry. They are not about to leave it because it is changing, even though they don't like and are frightened by the changes. They will have to learn to survive in a smaller pond by getting together with the crayfish.

Selling to Fewer Customers

"Tougher for inventors" seems to be the almost universal opinion of this industry consolidation. Officers of several U.S. game manufacturers were recently polled to find their opinions on the current trend. Larry Bernstein of Mattel Games gave the one exception to the question, "How will the mergers affect inventors?"

Bernstein said Mattel's merger with International Games will be positive for inventors because the merged company will be taking more products than the two separate companies would have. Their combined strength in the market will give them a competitive advantage over what they had separately. Bernstein also noted that the coupling of a non-promotional company with a promotional company such as Mattel will be positive for inventors.

Susan Adamo, Vice President of Research & Development for Pressman Toy, said many inventors with whom she spoke were concerned, even wary. Inventors will have fewer companies to pitch products to, Adamo said, so more inventors (professional) are going to storyboards and even verbal descriptions of a concept to gauge a manufacturer's interest. The mergers put Pressman in a good position she added because Pressman responds quickly to inventors.

Chris Campbell, Vice President of Marketing at Tyco Toys, agreed the mergers mean fewer opportunities for inventors. He viewed the merger trend in general as perhaps inevitable, but "not healthy" for inventors because of the resulting consolidation of power. However, he believed the mergers would create opportunities for Tyco. Campbell said the greater concern is the consolidation of power in retail.

"Is life imitating art?", was the question Lee Gelber of the Starting Nine asked as he joked about the trend approaching the ultimate conclusion of one manufacturer selling one retailer. His major concern regarding consolidation was the stakes will be higher in the promotional arena. Gelber said major buyers were concerned about the sizes of resulting game companies being cumbersome, which he felt created an opportunity for new companies. Other officers polled received similar comments from buyers and felt the concern does in fact create opportunities for new and smaller companies.

Barbara Allen of Cadaco said the wave of mergers seems to be a trend, which will make it tough on inventors. The greater concern for inventors and manufacturers alike, said Allen, is retailers are shrinking their SKU's (Stock Keeping Units—the number of different products in a store) in their desire to carry fewer items with higher turn rates (how quickly the item sells).

Jim Ward, Marketing Director for TSR, sees the merger trend as "terribly destructive." He likes competition and is unhappy with the number of competitors declining. Ward said manufacturers will probably make harder deals with inventors because there are fewer competitors.

There was no consensus on whether we would see additional mergers in the game industry. Bernstein said he did not foresee additional mergers since there were no other staple products to be acquired. Ward thought more mergers would be in the offing, and Campbell observed a few non-domestic manufacturers, such as Irwin and Chieftain, were entering the U.S. market. That's good news for inventors.

Ward did not see any new, domestic manufacturers emerging anytime soon, since the net cost of entering the industry at that level is substantially higher than it had been in the past.

Get the Picture?

No matter how you go about submitting an idea to a game company you had better know the industry—at least to the extent that you don't send a children's skill & action game to a company that is interested only in adult sports games.

TRY THIS GAME PLAN

What's the first possibility? Get an agent. Game agents are similar to literary and talent agents. They represent inventors' ideas to game companies for a percentage of the royalty. Many of the same game companies who will tell you they don't accept outside submissions from unknown inventors will turn right around and send you a list of agents authorized to show them product. Why and how to deal with agents is discussed in more detail later.

Trying to sell your idea without an agent means you have to become an established game inventor, with one or more games under your belt. This will give you an "in" when you make future proposals to game companies. Of course, this also creates a *Catch-22* scenario; how do you get that experience when no one will give you a job in the first place.

This brings us to your third possibility: Produce your own game. Market it with all the determination and enthusiasm you can muster. Then, when it has become moderately successful, submit a letter of inquiry to the game company you have targeted. Include with the letter a marketing brief detailing the history of the game's sales, including where it sold, retailers who sell it, and how much money has been spent to establish a foothold in the market. This method is your most practical way to get a large game company to look at your work. If that approach is not possible (not enough money, time or energy), there still is one avenue open.

Produce the game as cheaply as possible, even if it means as few as 100 copies at a quick copy printer. Make certain, however, to include the trademark symbol (™) by the title and the official copyright line on the box. Run a classified ad in the newspapers and beg any retailers you know to put the game in their outlets on a consignment basis. Then, dig in and deluge the game companies with letters and phone calls. If possible, visit them personally. Whatever you do, be persistent! Make it clear that the game has already been produced, regardless of the quality. The odds still are very much against success, but at least there is a chance someone will relent, show some compassion, and look at your work.

It is important to remember nearly all the blockbuster games were first produced as entrepreneurial ventures, became successful on their own, and *then* were bought by major companies.

DO PUBLISHERS HAVE TO BE SO TOUGH?

Why do major companies resist looking at outside submissions? Reasons can vary from firm to firm, but the three most common are legal expenses, time, and marketing.

No one likes to be sued. It's an unpleasant, ulcer-inducing experience that can cost thousands of dollars—even if you win. Since game companies always have a backlog of games in various stages of design and production, they have to be extremely careful when they consider outside submissions. They may decide to reject a game because it is similar to one already in development. When their own game hits the market, the freelance designer might see it, think the company has stolen his idea and get his attorney-cum-brother-in-law to file suit.

Don't shake your head in disbelief. It's a story that has been repeated over and over. Even if the company wins the suit, which they usually do (because of peculiar copyright laws governing board games), there still is the matter of tens of thousands of dollars in legal fees.

Time is another obstacle. If a company the size of Milton Bradley looked at every game that arrived in the morning mail, they would need two or three full time game analysts just to begin to evaluate just the few proposals that showed promise.

The third reason for resistance, marketing, may seem the strangest of all. Most major firms do employ a game designing staff, but you would be surprised how small these staffs are. The few people who manage to land these jobs don't sit around in an idyllic world dreaming up games. In many cases, it's the marketing staff who decide the subject and style of the projects. They do a thorough study, then send a memo to the design department advising the inventors of the needed requirements.

The intention might be to devise a game about three cartoon characters in a giant washing machine. It might have to be for four year olds, inoffensive to American Indians, playable in seven to fifteen minutes and packaged so that it can sell for $3.99. That retail price limits you to a small game board, a box, one die, and six playing pieces. What all this means, of course, is that even if a company does agree to look at a freelance game, if it doesn't work within current marketing plans, it is rejected—no matter how good it is.

Looking at it from their perspective, you are forced to agree there is a legitimate rationale underpinning the large companies' aversion to outside submissions. But what about the not-so-major companies? There are many more of them.

HOW ABOUT THE SMALL AND MEDIUM-SIZED GAME PRODUCERS?

Small to medium-sized companies are more open to accepting submissions if the game seems interesting and fits the parameters of their market. But, watch out! These companies generally do not have the money to pay advances, nor the need to do so. Designers need them a lot more than they need designers. They may do things like test marketing less than five thousand copies of a game. What this means for you is that even if the game does catch on, the chances are your royalties will not buy you a new car every fifth year.

What if you succeed in selling your game to a publisher? Well, once you do, it belongs to whoever bought it, body and soul. Sure, there's a royalty agreement, but what happens if the game attracts the attention of a major company and the smaller company sells it to them? If you signed a fairly standard contract, chances are you'll get royalties based on what the company receives from the resale. That means they are apt to wind up with 50% or more, and you are left trying to figure out what happened.

RULES FOR SUBMITTING GAMES

If you want to have any chance of getting companies to look at your game, follow this advice:

1. Never send a game—*under any circumstances*—until a company asks for it. If they do, they usually will require a signed release exempting them from blame for any conceivable event. Submitting unsolicited games or using certified mail for routine inquiries simply annoys people.

2. If the game has been produced in any form and is to be submitted as such, be sure to have the legal copyright line imprinted on the box, board, rules and any other printed matter. Check with an attorney or the U.S. Copyright Office for details.

3. When sending a letter of inquiry, keep it brief and to the point, but include the following: whether you have sold other games to other companies; the subject of the game you are submitting; the age range, length of playing time, length of rules (a word count); a list of components, and a statement that you have examined games produced by this particular company and feel your game falls within their standard component range.

A separate enclosure should have a thorough marketing summary sheet of the game's sales record and copies of ads and major coverage (reviews and any other media mentions). All this should be typed neatly, double-spaced, on a sheet containing your name, address, and telephone number. Do not send a form letter or a photocopy. And many companies and individuals find copy produced on a dot matrix printer difficult to read. You do not want to irritate or frustrate a potential buyer.

4. If at all possible obtain the name of the person who decides which games will be brought into the company for evaluation. This person is usually the head of product acquisitions. Use his or her name on all correspondence.

5. If you know anyone who is associated in any way with the toy and game industry on a national level, try to enlist that person's assistance to help you get a foot in the door.

6. Keep hammering! You may have to send dozens of letters and make scores of phone calls just to get someone to talk to you. Most people don't like to say NO. Since their company policy requires them to say it so often, they probably prefer not to get involved at all with anyone making an unsolicited game submission.

7. Consider finding and using an agent. A good one may want a large share of the royalty but you have a much better chance of selling the idea with an agent than without one. Besides, unless new math has changed things, half of something is better than all of nothing.

PART 4: Selling Your Idea

MY IRISH FRIEND

Herbie Brennan and I have been friends for nearly twelve years but only recently met face to face. Herbie and I corresponded and chatted over the phone for years. Last year I traveled to his 200 year old home in Ireland and shared a bottle of fine Irish whiskey with him. He is primarily a writer, with fifty or so books to his credit, ranging from management guides to fantasy novels. He also is a business consultant, a partner in a direct marketing firm, a former advertising agency executive, an astrologer, acupuncturist, herbalist and just about every other kind of "ist" there is.

I am telling you about him because he's a game inventor who has been fortunate enough and smart enough to sell his games to other companies. I have imposed on our friendship to ask him, as an experienced invention/ideas marketer, to share his thoughts on selling a game to a publisher. The following pages are his contribution to your success in the game industry.

THE ROAD TO FAME AND FORTUNE

Yes sir, there are publishers out there—people who will take your idea, package it, market it and promote it—all at their own expense. As the game sells, they will pay you money in the form of royalties. In some instances, they may even be persuaded to pay you money in the form of an advance, before your game ever gets into the stores. It's an awful lot easier and much less risky than marketing your own game, however much you may learn in the following pages. But it has one drawback. Finding a publisher for that first game you have invented is like finding truffles in a French forest. You know the damn things are there all right, but you have to root around like crazy to unearth even one.

Just how difficult it is to find a publisher for a first game is underscored by the research Steve did before he started this book. He received only thirteen responses to fifty inquiries mailed to the largest board game companies—and he wasn't even asking anyone to look at a game.

The truth is that really big game companies are unlikely to touch you with a ten-foot pole. The small-to-medium-sized publishers might be interested in your wares, but your chances of a smash-hit marketing success with them are much less than with a huge publisher. Small companies just don't have the same distribution network or anything like the same promotional budget. If your game is a winner, however, and if it has that compulsive, addictive quality that keeps players coming back for more, then it's going to claw its way up through the marketplace. All it takes is a little bit of luck and a reasonable amount of business expertise. Your biggest problem, interesting a publisher, will hinge on a secondary problem of defining the product you are marketing with the utmost clarity.

Let's take that second problem first. Since games are invented in stages, you might simply come up with a brilliant idea and leave it at that, or you might work the idea through into a detailed concept. Maybe you'll go so far as to do sample design and artwork, in order to have a full-scale, professional-looking prototype to tuck under your arm. You may already have produced and marketed your own game, and now wish to try to interest a publisher in taking the ball and running with it — faster and further than you think you can on your own. Selling a publisher on your product requires a number of different techniques, depending upon the stage in your game's development at which you choose to make your move.

THE PERILS OF IDEAS

There is a market for ideas. It is a risky and difficult market, and unlikely to make you wealthy, but it does exist. To get anywhere at all, you will need to hold two strong cards for openers; the ideas themselves and the ability to express them persuasively. Then you'll need patience, perseverance, a thick skin, a hard nose, and a good lawyer.

This is a market rich in legal quicksand, for copyright protection of an idea (as opposed to the expression of that idea) is nearly impossible to establish. The net result: when you try to sell an idea, you run a very real risk of having it stolen, with no legal recourse whatsoever. For this reason you'll find that *everybody* in the ideas market is seriously paranoid. But try it anyway. You might even enjoy it. Some people wrestle alligators for a living.

The strangest thing is that the most paranoid people of all will be the people to whom you will have to offer your ideas. The very ones you should fear may take your vision and run are the ones most disturbed by the fact that your "baby" does not have any clear cut legal protection.

WHY IS EVERYONE SO PARANOID?

Ideas float freely in the air, waiting to be picked like fruit. You can bet that the most ingenious notion you have ever had will be shared by someone, somewhere. Since the world is a mighty big place, the emergence of the same idea in different locations rarely creates conflicts, indeed often fails even to attract notice. Take the theory of evolution, for instance. It was a pretty extreme notion when it occurred to Darwin, but not so far out that Wallace didn't think of it at the same time. There was no question of collusion. History simply attests that these two great scientists somehow achieved a more or less identical intellectual breakthrough quite independently.

When it happens that two versions of the same idea come into headlong collision, however, people tend to reach for their attorneys as quickly as Wild Bill Hickok used to reach for his gun.

Put yourself in the position of the president of a big company. You have your own research and development team, funded by a multi-million dollar budget. This team comes up with potential new products all the time. Most of these fail to pass a limited market test. Nonetheless, the team continues to brainstorm and conceive. Right now they are working on the greatest game since ...

In the midst of these continuing creative explosions, your secretary brings you the morning's mail. In the pile is a letter from a middle-aged schoolteacher in Columbus, Ohio outlining substantially the same hot idea your R&D team is currently developing. The teacher thinks it is a good notion and wants you to make her an offer.

You spot problems right away. You are not about to waste company money paying for an idea your own team has already hit upon. At the same time, you can see that the teacher is not going to believe you when you tell her she's too late. The minute your letter reaches her, stating your men had the idea first, she is going to sue. She may not win the suit, but that doesn't matter. The very fact that she mounts a legal action will cost you time and money, and bring you bad publicity. It's a no-win situation no matter the final judgment.

GAME SUBMISSIONS OFTEN ARE RETURNED UNOPENED

It's such a no-win situation that major corporations (inside and outside the game industry) just will not sit still for it. Submissions are returned unopened, if possible, or unread beyond the point where it becomes obvious you are about to tell them your idea.

However, some corporations do not go quite that far. Their executives harbor the distant hope that somewhere out there somebody might just have an idea that will make money. They want to consider outside submissions, but they don't want to end up in a legal mess, so they implement a killer policy—"killer", that is, from the standpoint of the outside game inventor.

The first step in this strategy is to announce that no ideas will be considered unless preceded by a letter requesting permission to submit the idea. The second step is for the company to send you a legally binding contract to sign.

This contract, when it arrives, has nothing at all to do with your idea (which, of course, you have not yet submitted). Instead, it is a document absolutely freeing the corporation from any responsibility whatsoever for what they may do with your idea when you do submit it. It's a document attesting to your relinquishment of all rights to your idea, and it pledges to you take no legal action against the corporation even if they steal it. In short, it's a document that eliminates every legal right you have, and places you in a position of absolute trust vis à vis the corporation.

Believe it or not, I have signed such documents. I didn't like it, but I could not see any more viable options. At the same time, I am pleased to report I have never been cheated by a corporation. It's sort of like the mechanism a dog will use when he gets into a fight that's too much for him. He will roll over submissively and offer his throat. At this point the big dog savaging him usually loses interest and backs off.

I'm not advocating that you sign every such killer contract that comes your way. What I am saying is that if you are in the ideas market you have to be realistic and recognize the other fellow has his problems too. If the company issuing the contract is well established and respectable, then the chances are they are only being cautious and are not trying to steal your brilliant notion. However, contracts of this type issued by an unknown corporation, or by one with a reputation for sharp practices, should be dumped in the garbage.

WHEN TO SIGN A CONTRACT

What it all comes down to is this. If you can find a corporation that will consider your idea without forcing you to sign the sort of contract Faust made with Mephistopheles, count yourself lucky and send them the idea. If an established company requires you to sign, do so. The chances are you will come out with a whole skin. However, you should also be aware that even if they don't steal your idea, you have given them an unquestionable edge when it comes to working out the payment agreement. In effect, legally they can pay you anything they want—or nothing at all. Most corporations are fair when it comes to payment, but none are all that fair. You are going to be a bit disappointed in the deal you get eventually.

If a company known or perceived as shady insists you sign the contract, don't. If you keep looking, you may find someone better, more reliable. Or you may eventually find yourself in a position to market the idea yourself.

DECIDING ON YOUR PRESENTATION

Now it's time to take a long hard look at your game and the form in which to present it.

In some industries, the most basic idea is worth money in its own right. Several years ago I acted as agent for a British inventor who came up with a very interesting notion for manufacturers of audio cassette tapes. At that time, cassette manufacturers used plain leader tapes. The inventor's bright idea was to replace this leader with tape that cleaned the recording head: a simple concept and one that I thought had marketing potential.

As things turned out, it earned no money for the inventor and no commission for me. The company to whom the idea was submitted declined to buy it on the grounds that auto-cleaning sound tapes would not have public appeal, and that such tapes would interfere with their sales of special head-cleaning cassettes.

In marketing terms the company was wrong on the first point and right on the second. Auto-cleaning tapes are now on the market and their added value aspect has made them popular with cassette users.

They are so popular, in fact, the profits from increased sales far outweigh the losses experienced in the area of specialized head-cleaning cassettes.

SOMETIMES TIME IS OF THE ESSENCE

None of this was of any use to the British inventor, however. While we were still promoting the idea, an overseas company introduced it commercially. There was no question of theft. As I said earlier, good ideas float about in the air. To make money from them, you have to be not just imaginative but quick and lucky as well.

An idea as simple as this might have potential in some fields but, I regret to report, the game industry is not one of them. Game publishers are up to their ears in good ideas, and most of them have been used in one form or another. What they want, if they want anything at all, is a developed proposal. They believe (quite rightly in my opinion) that just about every worthwhile idea has been tried in some way. The crucial success factor is the specific implementation.

When it comes to boxed games the presentation of your idea has to be pretty thorough. You have to have the rules in final form and give a very clear indication of how the board should look, what sort of pieces your game requires and so on. A brief synopsis is useless. In this area, you are no longer really marketing a rough idea. To all intents and purposes you are creating a prototype of your new game.

There is, however, one sector where underdeveloped ideas are still welcome and that is the volatile home computer game industry.

A BYTE INTO THE SOFTWARE MARKET

Over the past decade computer games have enjoyed an upsurge in popularity so great they have made many entrepreneurs quite wealthy. Consequently, more and more hopeful companies are attracted to this market, producing a flood of look-alike, me-too software. As the competition heightens, software houses become increasingly desperate for programs that will help them capture large chunks of the market.

Such corporations have a fundamental problem. The creation of a computer game requires two very separate skills; the ability to program and the ability to design a worthwhile game. Rare is the individual endowed with both these skills, so many software corporations are willing—and some actually anxious—to listen to computer game ideas, even if it's obvious you can't tell a PEEK from a POKE. This can be a lucrative market, but bear in mind there are a few caveats.

Just as in the board game market, larger software houses have their own creative departments and are much less interested in outside submissions (in idea form) than their smaller competitors. Also, the sad truth is that the software industry has more cowboys in it than Boot Hill, and more crapshooters than in Las Vegas and Atlantic City combined. You need to take special care to pick a small company with some track record, not one that opened its doors yesterday and may well close them tomorrow.

Selecting a reputable target company in this sector is far from easy, but there are some helpful guidelines. You might, for example, study their advertising. Cheap, amateurish advertising indicates a cheap, amateurish company. Limited advertising suggests a company that is short on capital. Both are bad news for you as a prospective ideas marketer. Consequently, it's important to look at a sample of the company's products. There is a great deal of rubbish software on the market. If their standards are low, you are well advised to avoid that particular company.

The final consideration is how much the company will promise you for your idea. This is the trickiest part of all because—paradoxically—the higher the offer, the less likely it is that you are getting a sound deal.

I have in my files a collection of bizarre advertisements from a variety of software houses offering rewards of $50,000 plus for game programs and program ideas. Some promise royalties as high as 35%. This may sound like a dream about to come true, but chances are it is not. Tired old cliches usually are true, and there is no such thing as a free lunch.

Even in the overpriced software market you need a lot of sales to generate $50,000, in addition to the profit the software house needs to retain. Unless your idea is strong and attractive enough to generate mass sales, you will not earn big rewards, no matter how fervently they have been promised. Software corporations are not charitable institutions. The big royalties they may promise are always tempting, but there is a level at which they become unrealistic to everybody, and basic business considerations must take over. Like any other product, a game is a commercial success only if its income exceeds the costs incurred to produce and market it; a 35% royalty calculated retail or wholesale will overwhelm any cost/income analysis I have ever seen.

Computer Game Packaging

Assuming you have managed to avoid the cowboys and crapshooters and have found a software house anxious to consider your game ideas, there still is the question of packaging—an element of your presentation that may be as important as the product itself. Even the best ideas require good packaging if they are to sell; in other words, you should take the time and trouble to present the product properly.

Let's look at a concrete example of ideas presentation.

In 1980, while suffering from exhaustion caused by playing *SPACE INVADERS* excessively, I decided it would be fun to have my own computer game on the market. The hitch was that I had almost no idea how to program a computer. This set me back to creating and selling a game program idea. There was no way I could cobble together even a rough simulation of how it would look on a screen, so I had to package it in such a way as to appeal to a software house.

My basic idea arose out of market analysis. It was obvious at the time that the bestselling home computer games were of the shoot 'em up, arcade variety. It also was fairly obvious to me that the market for arcade games was overcrowded and the boom in sales could not last forever.

A closer look at the situation yielded additional insight. While arcade games were the super-sellers, there was another category of home computer games far less influenced by novelty and fashion. These games continued to enjoy steady sales. Games in this category were computerized versions of old favorites such as backgammon, checkers, and

Mah Jong. Many of these games had been around for years in computer form and some had been popular board games for centuries.

My idea was to take a traditional game — one that promised lasting appeal — from this category and combine it with an arcade game. I hoped the combination would add novelty, excitement . . . and sales.

Now that may seem like an exciting enough notion to you but I doubt that you would rush to put money on it. It is an idea but it's a broad idea, one that needs refining before it can become a viable commercial entity.

The traditional game I selected for this great transformation was chess. Now I don't suppose that impresses you too much; there are many fine chess programs on the market and more being developed every day. But if you're yawning now, you may be a lot more interested to learn how I packaged this notion for presentation to a software house. The next section gives that presentation in its entirety.

DEATHCHESS 5000: A Computer Game Proposal

Background

Because of the challenges it presents, chess has long been of interest to computer programmers. Early attempts to translate the board game into a computer game had limited results, but today there are several interesting chess programs on the market, presenting analysis of the moves to a greater or lesser depth.

New versions still are being produced, with the promotional emphasis on the "more powerful than..." approach. Chess programs play chess programs and the winner is hailed in the promotional material.

Sales of chess programs are, by definition, confined largely to chess players. It had been difficult to envision a chess program with the broad market appeal of, for example, a good arcade game.

Until now ....

Deathchess 5000

Deathchess 5000 is seen as a game program with a market appeal far beyond that of orthodox chess. Although not necessarily structured in levels of accomplishment, it is the sort of game that can be enjoyed by players of any skill level, from novice to grand master.

More importantly, it actually can be played and enjoyed without any knowledge of chess whatsoever. I must admit, though, that a knowledge of chess strategy and tactics would tend to raise the game dramatically.

Deathchess: An Overview

Deathchess 5000 would become the first computer game to combine an orthodox chess program with arcade game elements.

The combination produces an entirely new type of game, with opportunities to develop strategies very different from those of the original board game. Played to its fullest potential, it would embody elements of action and excitement in addition to the purely intellectual delights of orthodox chess.

-2

In essence, Deathchess 5000 would take us back to the roots of chess itself which, as Chatjuranga, was one of the earliest and most popular battle simulations ever devised.

The Program Described

As presently projected, the final program would present itself to a player in the following form:

Titles

The program opens on a starscape. Tumbling toward the player, growing larger as it approaches, is a transparent, 3-D line representation of a chessboard. Animation of the board ceases when it fills the screen, with the starscape still discernible through it. At this point, animated titles would crash superimposed, held over a short delay, then faded as the program moves on to the game itself.

Opening Game Sequence

A perfectly orthodox 64-square chessboard would appear on screen, set up with pieces to begin a game. Representation of the pieces could be the familiar Staunton shapes, but an added dimension might become the adoption of more novel "warrior" shapes to represent the pieces. There are pros and cons to both approaches. The Staunton pieces have the advantage of instant recognizability. A warrior design might prove confusing at first but would add to the overall atmosphere of the game.

Start of Play

Since the rules of the game are those of orthodox chess, the first move would be made by white. Again exactly like any other chess program on the market, the move would be made by keying in coded start and finish coordinates of the pawn or piece the player wishes to advance. The computer would naturally refuse to accept illegal moves, but given that the initial move is allowable, the computer (playing black) would make its own reply move. At this point, we are involved in a totally straightforward chess program.

-3

The Action Begins

The game will continue to play like orthodox chess until a pawn or piece is in a position to be taken. At this point the game abruptly changes character. To illustrate this, we can examine a pawn-take-pawn move.

As the pawn-take-pawn instruction is keyed in, the chessboard fades from the screen to be replaced by an enlarged graphic of a single square set out as a battlefield. On the battlefield are two animated warrior figures, one white and one black. Each is armed with a laser rifle. The black warrior is under the control of the computer, the white under player control.

The play is immediately placed in a real-time, arcade-style action situation in which the white (pawn) warrior must, through speed and skill, kill the black warrior or be killed. The animated battle would continue until it is resolved by the death of one pawn.

The Game Continues

Once the pawn-take-pawn warrior battle is finished, the game returns to the orthodox chessboard. The computer now stores in memory the result of the battle and accepts that as the outcome of the particular move. In other words, while white may set out to take a black pawn, white only succeeds in doing so if his warrior defeats the black warrior. If the white warrior is defeated, the game continues as if black had taken white, rather than vice versa.

Follow Through

The potential of this approach is limited only by computer memory and programmer imagination. Ideally, different styles of fights are foreseen: wizard battles between bishops; tank battles between rooks; mounted battles between knights (mounted on personal flyers rather than horses in this futuristic setting). Since a knight will not always battle a knight, of course, but may have to face a pawn, bishop, rook, or even queen, each piece would require fundamentally different armaments and possibly movement factors—to simulate the relative strengths of the actual pieces.

Nevertheless, in this version of chess, a pawn warrior might just win over an attacking knight warrior if the player is fast enough and skillful enough.

-4

Program Considerations

The following consideration should be borne in mind in relation to the playability of the game:

1. Whatever the relative strengths, an attacking piece or pawn should be given a distinct edge over a defender. This enables much of normal chess strategy to be retained. How substantial an edge is allowed will obviously affect the overall play of the game and this is an area open to experiment during program development in order to produce the most addictive version.

2. Unlike orthodox chess, Deathchess 5000 cannot be won on a mate (which only threatens to take the opposing king in circumstances where the threat cannot be neutralized). Instead, the game is won when the opposing king is actually killed. Here again it will be important to find the optimum "battle strength" of the kings during program development.

3. Skeleton program development could almost certainly be built on an existing chess program. This need not (in fact, probably should not) be an advanced program, since the new game elements would totally overshadow any necessity for sophisticated in-depth play.

4. If possible, an option should be built in for a player vs. player game (possibly using joysticks), in addition to the basic player vs. computer version.

That, word for word, was the presentation of the idea which subsequently netted me a contract with Artic Computing Ltd., a major British software company. They followed the commonplace practice of offering a lump sum for outright sale of the idea, or a royalty percentage on the game as eventually produced. Given that the figures are agreeable, both are valid offers. However, I personally would opt for the royalty percentage (and did so in this case), unless I had an immediate cash need.

A royalty contract is a gamble. If the game fails to sell well, you earn little or nothing. On the other hand, if it turns out to be a second *PACMAN* you can make a great deal of money.

The format of the *Deathchess* presentation bears closer examination, since it incorporates certain factors pertinent to the process of submitting game ideas—as well as fully developed games—for publication. These factors will be analyzed in the next section.

SELLING SECRETS

It could be useful for you to read through Herbie's *Deathchess* 5000 proposal a second time. While it is not perfect, it did sell, and it sold for reasons that have little to do with the central idea.

In fact, Herbie's proposal was based on a variety of criteria not specifically relevant to the *Deathchess* game. Consequently, these criteria are applicable to any idea or developed game one might wish to sell to a publisher.

It Must Have Profit Potential

The first and most important of these criteria is a clear understanding of the prospective publisher's motivation. I am fairly familiar with the book publishing business, where it is still possible to find publishers whose primary interest is quality of product. Because their primary concern is publishing literature, they are willing to accept books that have literary merit even though the limited sales of such books will consign them to commercial failure.

At the risk of sounding insulting, I personally have never found a game publisher who was interested in anything other than the commercial success of his games. This probably is a good thing, since I also never have met a professional game designer with any other interest either. Games are games. Sometimes they are used for educational purposes, but basically they exist to entertain and amuse. They generally have no pretensions about being works of art. In the game business, commerce is king.

As a game designer, your primary focus lies in getting your game published. Game publishers, however, produce new games every year. The thrill of seeing yet another colorful box in print has long since worn off for them. What interests the publisher—first, last, and only —is whether a particular game has money-making potential. It doesn't necessarily have to be great money-making potential. Publishers are, after all, realists who recognize that huge successes like *MONOPOLY* and *Trivial Pursuit* do not land on their desks every day. However, it must show some commercial promise.

Recognition of this fact is the first step on the path toward commercial success; i.e., selling a publisher your game. It is pointless to tell him how wonderful the game is unless you first tell him (one way or another) how likely it is to achieve some success in the market. In telling him this you must build credibility.

The psychological dynamics of business relationships are very curious. Personal relationships may develop at their own pace, so to speak, and ripen like pieces of fruit. In business there seldom is time for this luxury. Judgments have to be made and made quickly. Such judgments are made on the basis of impressions—all too often, first impressions.

Pigeonholing For most people in business, impressions are formed (or profoundly influenced) by a process known as pigeonholing. You meet someone in a business context and, quite instinctively, seek a convenient mental pigeonhole in which to put that person. Your contact becomes a salesperson, an accountant, executive or whatever. You realize, of course, that the label on the pigeonhole may not tell the whole story, but it is a starting point and one that allows you to deal with the other person conveniently.

The problem with all this is that while you are neatly pigeonholing those you meet in business, they are quietly engaged in exactly the same process with you. Most companies play this game instinctively and show great concern not only for the collective corporate image, but also for the image presented by individual personnel. This is why salesmen often dress as conservatively as the chairman of the board, while the artists employed by advertising agencies often look like French impressionists. In the first instance, the salesmen are striving for respectability. In the second, the artists are attempting to be pigeonholed as "creative" individuals.

How you are pigeonholed depends, almost entirely, on the image you present. This is something worth thinking about before you approach a potential game publisher. A creative image is dramatic and attention-getting, but I personally have found it far more useful to project a hard-nosed image of marketing expertise. Publishers, who are marketing people themselves, feel at home with other marketing people. Once you are pigeonholed as a marketing expert, you cease to be looked upon as just another creative character with a bizarre game idea. Instead you are perceived as the producer of a product that has commercial potential. A marketer's image is no guarantee that a publisher will buy your game, but if the image is successfully projected, it will virtually guarantee your proposal at least will be carefully considered.

If you reread Herbie's *Deathchess* proposal in light of these comments, you will discover quickly it is written from a marketer's viewpoint. The opening section, entitled "Background", has used the word "market" by the second paragraph and talks about market appeal by the fourth. Even before you get into the description of the game itself, its potential appeal is being hyped ("far beyond that of orthodox chess") and you are psychologically set up to make a positive buying decision.

The proposal's short overview emphasizes that a new type of game is being offered. After all, novelty has a market appeal all its own. The overview further specifies that this game falls into both the long-selling chess and fast-selling arcade game categories. (It might be worth mentioning at this point that the *Deathchess* proposal was offered at a time when arcade games were still super-sellers in the British market, despite the fact that they had taken something of a tumble in the U.S.)

The format of the proposal is businesslike and methodical, reinforcing a professional image. The style is enthusiastic, but not overly so. Too many good ideas have been lost to overkill. The object was to write a "businessman to businessman" proposal. Such an approach usually commands more respect than an emotional hard-sell from a "creative" designer. When viewed in this light, the game itself becomes secondary.

The question of image goes far beyond whether you project yourself as a marketer. Such a projection happens to be one of my favorites (possibly because I am a marketer in many aspects of my career) but I'm aware it is not the only effective image. A track record as a successful game designer would be just as good, if not better. So would professional recognition in some other industry or profession.

No matter what image you wish to present, your proposal must be professional. Satisfying this criterion is essential, whether you are marketing a fully developed game or just a bare idea.

Now that a proposal's inner workings have been detailed let's look at another. This one is for a board game that is a little more up to date.

DATE! MATE!

The Battle-of-the-Sexes Date 'em or Mate 'em Game

Presented by

Game Plan, Inc.

DATE! MATE!

The Battle-of-the-Sexes Date 'em or Mate 'em Game

Audience

Though originally aimed at single adults only, extensive playtesting demonstrated:

- Married couples had as much fun.
- Senior citizens (married or single) loved it.
- Teenagers were drawn to it as the Spin-the-Bottle of the twenty-first century.
- DATE! MATE! appeals to ages fourteen and older.
- DATE! MATE! appeals to a wide demographic cross section of income, education, ethnic background, and interests.

DATE! MATE!

The Battle-of-the-Sexes Date 'em or Mate 'em Game

Appeal
- DATE! MATE!'s strong appeal stems from actual dating.
- Dating is a powerful and universal force in our culture.
- National interest in dating and love is reflected in non-stop stories in newspapers, magazines, and television as well as in pop music.
- The subconscious desire to appeal to the opposite sex is always present. The fantasy of enhancing this appeal is central in marketing and advertising.

Though not the least bit suggestive, DATE! MATE! plays to the fantasy aspects of this desire to appeal.

- DATE! MATE! innocently creates the element of the hunt, the excitement of the chase.
- It stimulates social interaction, lowering inhibitions.
- It makes people laugh and feel closer.
- Everyone can relate to the game.

DATE! MATE!

The Battle-of-the-Sexes Date 'em or Mate 'em Game

Game Play
- DATE! MATE! is different.
- Interaction—players 'date' all other players
- Directly involves more than one player most turns
- Whispering element allows players to place part of themselves in the game.
- Not a trivia, information or coordination based game where the smartest or most skillful usually wins
- Fast playing—game length controlled by scoring
- Encourages and permits social interaction which would not occur without the game. It's a license to have fun and excitement.
- Good dates, bad dates, Passion Points, humorous character pawns, secret whispers, Bachelor Heaven and the Wedding Chapel all enhance the pseudo role playing fantasy.

DATE! MATE!

The Battle-of-the-Sexes Date 'em or Mate 'em Game

Promotable
- DATE! MATE! will have strong television commercial appeal.
- Facial expressions induced by secret whispering provide visual intrigue and suspense.
- Passion Points in the shape of kisses, Bachelor Heaven, Wedding Chapel and fun character pawns (e.g., UPS delivery man, construction worker, police woman, etc.) provide strong visual allure.
- Game concept of Bachelor Heaven versus Wedding Chapel has universal, natural appeal. At the same time, DATE! MATE! provides a fresh approach.
- High level of player interaction and involvement will be easy to portray realistically.

DATE! MATE!

The Battle-of-the-Sexes Date 'em or Mate 'em Game

Publicity

- DATE! MATE! can generate enormous publicity.
- Topic has universal appeal
- Daytime television talk shows with female audiences continuously revisit the subjects of dating and love
- Radio talk shows are starved for subjects to which the majority of their audiences can relate
- Inventor has strong entertainment background
- Inventor has audience appeal
- Inventor's 175 dating experiences inspired the game.

Did you notice there is very little in the DATE! MATE! proposal that addresses how the game works. While this particular game did not sell, the reason the proposal is used as an example is that it eventually found its way into the hands of product acquisition heads of a dozen companies. Based on the strength of the proposal, every one of them requested the game be submitted.

The proposal is a tool to get a foot in the door and work up enough interest to have them ask to see your game. Put a lot of time and creativity into your proposal. Remember, it's likely a great game introduced by a terrible proposal will never be seen.

A WORD ABOUT GAME AGENTS

About once a day an enthusiastic game inventor calls to ask if I can recommend a game agent to present his or her game to prospective publishers. Like literary agents, game agents sell clients' works for a share of the royalties. They differ from their literary cousins in that legitimate game agents are about as hard to find as publishing contracts and the game agent is likely to spend much more time and money developing your idea into a salable item.

Buyer Beware!

There are those agents, however, who prey on starry-eyed beginners. They have companies that take your game, conduct a three-day market study, and generate a fill-in-the-blank computer presentation to "sell" your idea to a game manufacturer. They will do all this for you for a modest up-front fee; perhaps $500 or more. In the unlikely event they get lucky and a publisher really does read and/or buy their stale proposal, they also want a percentage of the royalty.

I do not want to generalize and say that all such marketing and market research firms are worthless. Legitimate ones can be invaluable. However, I have yet to meet anyone who sold his game or game idea to a publisher by paying this type of firm to represent him.

If you are considering taking this path, be sure to be careful. Check out the firm first. Ask to see a list of actual games they have sold in the past. Then ask for a corresponding client list you can call, to learn first-hand what kind of firm they are before you part with any money.

It is possible to get lists of legitimate agents by writing letters to game companies asking if they maintain a list of agents authorized to show product, or by contacting Game Inventors of America. If an agent agrees to look at a design from a new inventor, then attempts to sell it and is successful, the inventor can expect to pay the agent about half the future royalties. On the positive side, legitimate agents rarely ask for money in advance except to cover specific expenses.

Why You Should Consider Agents

As you have discovered, being properly rewarded for selling a game idea is not easy. In addition to facing what appears to be a closed door policy, new inventors lack experience and the industry information necessary to achieve their goal—developing and selling a game to a major company.

Legitimate agents constantly meet with manufacturers to discuss their needs in today's ever-changing market. With that knowledge they fine-tune or radically transform a relatively sound but unsalable idea into a product tailored to fit manufacturers' requirements.

These transformations are evolutionary and expensive. Each advance is paid for by valuable creative time as well as cash outlays for prototype developments. Because legitimate agents (only paid a commission if successful) spend their own money, they are extremely selective in choosing products in which to invest their time and resources. A typical established agency receives a thousand invention proposals a year. From these, ten to twenty are accepted for representation.

Most submissions are good games. But in today's market good is not enough. Whether we like it or not, agree or not, game companies call the shots as to what they will or will not publish. Chess or checker variants, sports or gambling games might be great games, but if the manufacturers will not even consider them they are a waste of an agent's time. Agents are looking for good games that are salable in the current market.

A Leap of Faith

If your product is selected there are numerous advantages to working with agents but your decision to contract with any agency is a leap of faith. You must believe you are dealing with honest professionals who are among the best in their industry.

It's very likely a good agent will want to change your idea. Don't make the mistake of being married to a single concept. Think of your idea as a seed from which a product will grow. Whether it grows a single stem, a tall stalk, or a tree with many branches, the final product is apt to bear little resemblance to the seed from which it came. The final product is judged only by its ability to bear fruit. Professional inventors welcome suggestions for changes and improvements. It is an easy way to make a good idea better or a better idea great.

Finally, think of agents as the bridge between inventors and manufacturers. Once you have crossed the bridge and are known in the land of game makers, you no longer need the bridge. You will be privy to the same inside information the agent uses to help sell products.

LAST WORDS ON SELLING YOUR GAME

If your goal is to sell your game to an existing publisher, you have set a tough, but not impossible, task for yourself. Persistence and a professional, creative approach are the necessary tools. You may have to use several approaches several times with a number of different publishers. Don't allow yourself to become discouraged or gun-shy about contacting potential game houses. If you are creatively persistent, and you are trying to promote a product that has market potential, keep pitching. If the fast ball doesn't get the job done, try the slider or change-up.

How tough is it really? There are two rumors floating around about how a couple of ingenious game inventors managed to get big firms to look at, and eventually accept, their games. The first man, so the story goes, had tried everything. Determined not to waste any more postage he took vacation time and drove to his targeted game company's headquarters. He made a sandwich sign saying "Take Pity, Look At My Game!", draped it over his shoulders and greeted the company's employees and executives as they drove in to work in the mornings. The second fellow allegedly "borrowed" a well-known name from the game industry and illegally used it as an endorsement for his product. If the story is correct, he got his game published. However, if he loses the resulting lawsuit he will be destitute.

One final ploy a friend told me about may work as well for you as for the guy who dreamed it up. A man involved in selling investment plans through direct mail advertising would type a letter and send it to a prospective client. If he didn't get a response within three weeks, he would type an exact duplicate of the letter, then wad it up as if it had been placed in the trash. Next he would smooth it out and, using a bold marker, write across the top, "Please do not throw this away again." Then he sent it back to the name on the mailing list.

It's crazy, but it got attention in a creative way. If you are to have any success at all in getting a major company to examine your game, you must be creative ... but never ignore the fine line between "cleverly creative" and "sickeningly cute."

There are a lot of people out there with game ideas, nearly as many as there are authors of the (as yet unwritten) Great American Novel. The competition is stiff and the odds are stacked against success. If you do become that one in a million and your game makes you wealthy, all I can say is congratulations and more power to you. You deserve everything you get.

Now if I could just get some book publisher to look at the Great American Novel I'm writing ...

PART 5: Self-Publishing

Now that I have taken you down the Yellow Brick Road to show you how to submit work to publishers, it's time to get back into my Wicked-Witch-of-the-East costume. I am assuming (I hope incorrectly) that you have been unable to sell your game to a publisher but are still determined to see it given a chance in the marketplace. That means doing it yourself. Here goes then. The first step is to answer this question:

SHOULD I REALLY DO IT?

To decide whether a game is worth making, first do some homework. Determine if it is similar to others already on the market.

Product viability was discussed in the chapter on inventing. The process required here is similar but you are looking from a slightly different perspective. In the first process you were trying to determine if the idea was viable relative to selling it to a game manufacturer. Now you are examining the idea to see if it is worth bringing to the marketplace yourself. Cutting through the nuances, the real difference is this. Major game companies are not product category innovators. They are product category exploiters.

Trivial Pursuit opened up a new category of adult social interaction games. *DUNGEONS & DRAGONS* established the concept of commercial role playing games. *UNO* pioneered the true family card game genre. In short, while virtually all the blockbuster games of the last fifty years created a new product category, none of them originated in an established game company. This means that if your game does not neatly fit into an established category, your task is to try to determine if there is a market for the product ... not to see if an existing company is interested in marketing it.

FINDING A FRIENDLY RETAILER

People in the gaming industry are deluged with new games every day, but few of them are unique, or even truly distinctive. Search hard enough and you will find games like your own, although you hope none will be too similar. Once you have been able to ascertain this, find out how well the games did. Usually this can be accomplished by getting friendly with merchants who have sold games for a number of years. Locate one with a good memory and a "willing to be helpful" personality, and he or she will provide a wealth of information. In most cases retailers remember only two types of games: those that sold extremely well and those that did not sell at all.

You may find games like your own still being sold. The simplest way to check this is to go into stores that have a decent supply of board games. Spend some time there examining the stock, making sure you read the backs of the boxes. Once you have identified several games as being similar to your design, try to obtain copies. Find out who made them. Check the copyright date, then look for the latest edition or printing. Find out how well the games sold, or are selling. Try to find advertisements for the game. Ask friends, family, and neighbors if they ever have heard of or played the game. Remember, if it is similar, this feedback will give you valuable clues as to how your game is going to be received.

Once you have studied some of these other games, get people (not family) to play them. Captive audiences who instinctively are on your side simply will not give you any valid insights. If the game is similar in subject matter, have your testers play it alongside yours. You will be surprised by how much information you can pick up just by paying attention to the attitudes of those asked to participate.

While the testers are playing, just relax and enjoy the game. Make it enjoyable for others. Don't make constant comparisons to your own game. After play is finished, analyze the game relative to your own. Determine the ways in which your game is better as well as ways in which your game could be improved.

DEFINE YOUR MARKET

The next step is to study the market. This requires more research. Start by defining the theme or subject matter of your game. For instance: *MONOPOLY* has real-estate as its theme. *Risk* offers an abstract world war background. *SCRABBLE* is a crossword puzzle game. Once the underlying theme has been identified, determine what and where its markets are going to be. Subjects with limited market appeal, like the game by the dog-breeding lady, offer the advantage of attracting small groups of easily-targeted people likely to be interested in the product at a reasonable cost. Mass market appeal items have a much wider population on which to base sales but it is much more expensive to reach their diverse audiences.

Once you have tagged your game with a theme and have been able to identify its market, put it under a mathematical microscope to determine its sales potential and the best marketing approach. How many people are there in the specific market? What percentage of them would be interested in buying the game? Are they mostly men, women, children, or a combination? What age group is involved and what is the average income? Where do these people shop? What magazines do they read? What television shows do they watch?

SOME NECESSARY MARKET RESEARCH

Hypothesize for a few minutes. Let's say we are researching a game based on the American Civil War. This is a limited, specific interest market, which makes it easier to define. But it will be harder to generate mass sales, relative to a more general market. A quick trip to the local library enables you to identify half a dozen magazines devoted exclusively to this theme.

A couple of weeks later, after a few letters and phone calls, you get some advertising information from these magazines. You discover the largest, in terms of circulation, is the *Civil War Times Illustrated*. We find it has over 100,000 readers, a large enough base to make analysis meaningful. After all, the circulation of all the Civil War magazines, allowing for duplication, is about 300,000.

The demographics of the magazines indicate the average reader is a 38-year-old male, with an annual income of $42,000. So far so good, right? Maybe! This man does not sound like a person who plays many games. But, suppose our man is married, has 1.7 children and spends a great deal of time reading, writing, and participating in other indoor activities. The magazine's promotional material should tell you this. If you are lucky the demographics might even reveal how many of these men play board games. Some magazines include this question in their survey forms.

Now you know the consumer to whom your ads should be directed. Thumbing through back issues of the magazine, and keeping notes on the kinds of ads that appear—especially those that are repeated in issue after issue—you can determine what appeals best to the readers. If you spot an ad for another game about the Civil War, don't panic. I said very few games are unique. Instead, write down the name and address of the company. Contact the company to order the game or look for it in stores. If no store within a 100-mile radius has heard of it, chances are it is being produced by someone just like you.

Luckily, Game Inventors Love to Talk

That may be a break. People who publish their own games like to talk about them. Give the company a call after seeing (preferably playing) the game and finding something nice to say about it. Ask questions about the play and design. When the designer starts talking, tell him where you saw the ad and inquire about other ad placements. It is amazing how much information people will share.

So you found the ad, ordered the game, and called the person who produced it. He tells you, "Yeah, my CWT ad pulls okay, but the wargamers are really eating it up." "What," you ask, "are wargamers?"

Wargamers: A Large Group

He explains that wargamers are a group of people who play games about wars. With a little prodding, you get the names of six "wargame" magazines. A quick check of the library's guide to periodicals shows you that another market has just been discovered.

You contact these magazine publishers and receive more information. You estimate that this other market contains another 200,000 warm bodies, giving you a total of 500,000 potential customers who are already interested in the subject of your game.

Estimating the Size of the Market

Now you're getting somewhere! You have identified a universe of half a million people who are interested in the American Civil War to some extent, and 200,000 of them are known gamers. It looks as though you have struck pay-dirt! Let's apply a few rules of thumb to see where you really are.

Nearly every marketing or advertising book presents a set of formulas which are supposed to tell how to determine advertising response. None of them guarantee anything, of course, but they all claim to be fairly accurate. Not to be outdone, here is my own formula for results obtained from placing ads in specialized magazines. I have found it to be reasonably accurate; at least as accurate as the textbook approaches.

MAGAZINE READERS, AD READERS, AND GAME BUYERS

Approximately 10% of the readers of a magazine will read a full page ad. (If the ad is in color, the percentage will go up; if the ad is less than a full page, the percentage will go down.) Of the 10% who spend 30 to 60 seconds reading the ad, perhaps 1% will order the item—assuming it is competitively priced and looks like quality merchandise. Now, where does that leave you?

Ten percent of 500,000 is 50,000. One percent of 50,000 is 500. So, following the Peek Principle, if you have a good ad, a good product, and a decent price you could expect to sell 500 copies of the Civil War game by placing a full page ad in each of the magazines you have discovered. If most of these are mail order sales at full retail price, you should do okay. It used to be that only one out of every ten Americans ever ordered by direct mail, but that percentage has been increasing in recent years, stimulated by fuel price increases and the rising number of two-income households.

Finished? Not yet! Flip through the war game magazines looking at the kind of ads that keep recurring. Suddenly you spot yet another ad for another Civil War game, but this time in the classified section. Wondering why in the world wargame makers would advertise here, you scan the page and see an interesting little ad in the corner. It's about Civil War Reenactment groups; people who dress in Civil War uniforms from particular regiments and recreate particular battles. Now you have stumbled on another potential market. Starting to get the idea?

Read those magazines! Study them from cover to cover, inside and out. Not only can they identify new markets that might otherwise take you years to find, they also can lead to other magazines in those markets.

If you feel your game is not a special interest item and you don't need to go through all this, think again. You are missing a bet. Besides, unless you have enough money to start your own magazine, you don't have enough to advertise on television or in such general interest magazines as *Time, People,* or *Playboy.* In short, you have to start getting the game on the market someplace and you have to create enough beginning sales—and enough people playing and talking about your game — to generate some word-of-mouth advertising for the product.

SPACE ADVERTISING AND DIRECT MAIL SALES

A word of warning about direct mail sales. I have seen many clients awash in delusions of wealth as they sat punching potential sales into a calculator. Obviously there are a great many successful direct mail sales companies. The endless stream of catalogs that finds its way into our mail boxes is compelling evidence of that. However ... do not confuse being in the direct mail business with selling a single item by direct mail.

The difference between being in the direct mail business and selling something by direct mail is this. Direct mail companies can afford to spend a few dollars per sale for advertising because they know once you order the advertised product you are likely to order several more things from them. If you are running ads for a game and it is the only product you have to sell, then the relationship is over once you ship it to the customer. You either made a profit or you didn't. What this means is you have to aim direct mail ads to very specific audiences to be effective. Or, and this is the right way to do it, consider the money made from mail order sales as a subsidy for advertising the product in a particular publication.

Let's take another approach, with a game that has more general appeal. This time we have a game similar to *SCRABBLE* or *Boggle*. It's a word game, about as general as they come. Our task is to find places to advertise that will be relatively inexpensive, yet still reach a market with high interest potential. The first and most obvious places to investigate are the crossword and word puzzle magazines. Then think about other groups who are likely to be interested in words. There's MENSA, an organization whose members have extremely high IQs. I believe they have a mailing list of all their members, and I think someone once told me they run a wholesale operation and have a monthly newsletter.

What about writers and would-be writers? They have an intense interest in words and there are several popular writers' magazines. A special ad could be slanted for that market could be productive. And then there are ...

The point is, no matter what your game's theme, you should be able to identify, locate, and analyze potential markets. All it takes is a little imagination and intelligence—and a lot of research. If you don't seem to be making headway at first, or if you begin to get bored, just remember: the information you are gathering and analyzing is vital. Without it as a starting reference you are lost before you even begin.

CALLING ALL VENDORS

By now you have designed a game or at least have one in mind. You have found and categorized a number of markets, estimated the amount of advertising space you will need, and calculated the costs involved. You probably have played the game so often the family hides from you on Saturday nights. You're ready ... so what's next?

Working with Printers

It's time to make some preliminary phone calls to local printers, box makers, and board makers. You probably will find columns of their listings in the yellow pages. Be straightforward with them. After all, they are not sitting there just waiting to steal your idea. Ask them the exact dimensions of the largest game board they can make or have made and the same for the game box. There's no point in designing a game that can't be produced. However, you should bear in mind one fairly obvious consideration; the bigger the item, the more it will cost.

Be sure to ask the printers the size of the largest image area they can print. This is slightly smaller than the largest sheet they can run through their presses and represents the area where the ink is placed. A good standard sheet size is 28' by 40'. Most printers can handle this size, so make sure to design the components to a standard that will allow competitive bids. Once the sheet sizes are established, design every-thing to fit on as few sheets as possible. For example, if a game re-quires a deck of cards, change the size of the cards to get the deck on one press run. In printing the cardinal rule is: the fewer the press sheets, the less expensive the job.

If you are fortunate enough to live in an area near a printer who rou-tinely produces games, you probably will discover three things:

1. you will get a fair price and;

2. he will save you time, mistakes, and money by handling production entirely;

3. if your quantity is high enough, working with this printer probably will be the cheapest way to go.

On short runs you may pay a bit of a premium for this total capability, but it's better than your coordinating all the steps involved—from product assembly to storage. If you find someone like this, check him out first to confirm he does in fact produce games on a regular basis. If so, be grateful for your luck. (If you are planning to produce fewer than two thousand copies of the product, about the only way it will make economic sense is for you to do all the leg work and to contract individual components from smaller suppliers.)

Finding a Graphic Artist

Armed with this information, make a prototype, redoing the original if it is too large. List every item in the game (even the most obvious), beginning with the box. Failure to communicate to the artist *all* the el-ements involved could cost you a lot of extra money. You want to avoid every possible unnecessary expense.

Make sure you know all the elements in precise detail. For example: the quantity of each denomination of play money in your game; the size of the money; the number and size of any game cards; the number of tokens; the number of colors to print on the board, and whether the money will be printed on both sides or only one. Decide on the box top design. Will it be a color photograph, an illustration, or a multi-colored design? If the latter, in how many colors? Itemize every aspect of every component before taking it to show anyone.

Graphic artists and printers are busy people. If you show up and say— "Guys, I've got this game I want you to make. It's about so big, and the box has got to be real pretty, and the game is a heck of a lot of fun to play"—they are going to show you the door politely and give you the name of a competitor whom they would dearly love to see take on this job.

When you meet the person who is going to do your final artwork, have a finished prototype ready in the right size, and all the components done to the best of your ability. The artist will need these for reference. For initial discussions have several copies of your itemized list of components, showing sizes, numbers, and colors.

At this point, you should become a bit of a horse trader. If you're smart, you will find a commercial artist who doesn't have a fancy office (he or she might even work in a home-based studio) or a large ad in the yellow pages. You are not yet a big-time game producer. There is no point in paying for extra overhead.

Sit down with the artist and go over your entire list. Don't skip anything. Most artists tend to miss details until it comes time for them to make up their invoices. After you have discussed every item, including the method of doing four-color art for the board and box top, ask the artist to provide a quote for the entire job. If the artist refuses, or says he would rather charge by the hour, gather up your materials, say goodbye, and find another designer. You have come to the wrong place.

Computer Graphic Skills Important

Something else to look for in an artist is good computer graphic capability. Computer graphics have come a long way. An experienced creative artist/operater should be able to produce commercial quality art. One of the main reasons to do your art on a computer is that it eliminates an expensive step—turning the art into negatives. This can be done automatically with the right output devices. It will be worth your while to learn about and understand this capability.

Negotiating a Price

It will take several such interviews with different artists to obtain and determine the best price. Notice I didn't say the lowest price. Make sure you are comparing apples with apples when you are comparing estimates. Don't be misled just because one price is substantially lower than the others. On the contrary, be suspicious of very low bids. After settling on two or three fair quotes, go back to the artists and point out to them that this is a highly speculative venture. Make it clear your financial resources are limited, and suggest a trade-off: a price reduction in exchange for, say, six months lead time to finish the artwork. That would enable the artist to work on it during slow times. Sometimes this works, sometimes it does not. Assuming you can wait the six months, it's worth a shot.

A final but often overlooked criterion in selecting an artist is the need to find someone with whom you are comfortable. You are going to be spending a lot of time together. At some point you probably are going to have to be critical about some error in production. You want to be able to make your point without incurring the artist's wrath.

Box Design Is *Very* Important

When most people think of designing a game box, or any package for that matter, they ponder how they can make it beautiful. The graphic person involved will try to make it an award winning piece of graphic art. You are both right ... and you are both dead wrong. How can this be?

A package has an important mission. It helps if it is beautiful. It also helps if it has award winning graphics. But all of that is so much money wasted if the package is not *effective*. Before designing your package understand its mission. I am about to tell you what a package must do. If you want to have an edge, your package should do it better than the competing packages around it.

When people purchase things on impulse (they did not go into the store looking for the particular item they left with) they go through a ritual. If you don't believe this, watch a person buy a box of cereal next time you are in a supermarket.

Don't Neglect the Bottom of the Box

The ritual goes something like this. The consumer sees the game's end panel (side) and something captures his or her attention (color contrast appeal, title, theme, picture). He pulls the box from the shelf and looks at the top. He will spend four to seven seconds deciding if he should invest more time with the product. If the box top is appealing, promises fun, and is not intimidating, the consumer turns the box over and examines the back of the box. (If you have saved a nickel by not printing on the box bottom you are headed for disaster. The consumer *expects* something to be back there. If you disappoint him the box is going right back on the shelf.)

The box bottom is a "quick read" billboard selling the product. The average consumer will spend a few seconds skimming headlines, pictures, and examples deciding whether to buy the product. If the box back keeps her interest she will invest another 20-30 seconds in the decision process. Assuming she is still interested, the next part of the ritual has her turning the box around to look for the price sticker.

Once she knows the dollar amount, the typical consumer unconsciously "weighs" the package with her hands, deciding if the product *feels* as if it is worth the price. (If you don't believe this just watch people buy things.) If everything checks out to her satisfaction, the consumer places the item in her shopping cart and you have made a sale. If any part of the process fails the ritual test, you could be dooming a great game—*because* no one will buy the product to find out how good it really *is*.

Bottom line here is the box has to be more than beautiful and have more than award winning graphics. It has to be as perfect and effective a package as possible.

First, the basics: do not skimp on the box top, side panels, and back. These are the most important pieces of art in a game. The overall design of the box has to be strong; eye-catching enough to make people notice it and pick it out from all the other games surrounding it on the shelves. Once the potential consumer has the game in hand, the sell copy on the back of the box absolutely has to be able to convince him he has no choice but to buy it. It not only has to make him want it, it should make him feel he just can't live without it.

You and the artist, but especially *you*, should put a lot of thought into these areas. You should already have looked at hundreds of game boxes and decided on your basic design approach before meeting with a potential artist. Basic approach, however, implies flexibility. When dealing with a sensitive artist (and I have yet to find one yet who is not sensitive), I have found it works best to tell them what you envision—colors, ideas, concepts, and images—then let him go to work.

Don't give them complete freedom, but enough to allow him or her enough room to think of the work as his or her own creation. Artists are most happy when they are putting their creative talents to work with as little supervision as possible.

WORKING WITH AN ARTIST: A TRUE STORY

All of this reminds me of my first experience with an artist. I was living outside Atlanta, Georgia and was working on my very first game. I had gone in to see a printer, one of the biggest in Atlanta. His office was in an impressive five-story building near the downtown area. I was taken into an elegant conference room and waited for my assigned agent. (They didn't call them salesmen in this place.)

He came in wearing a very expensive suit, a stylish haircut, and manicured nails. Offering me a drink, he pulled out a hidden bar from inside one of the walls. When he sat down I began to talk. "I've got this game," I said. "It's about this big and gee whiz, is it ever a lot of fun to play." He listened to me for a few minutes, nodding his head and looking at his watch. When I finished he told me he would be right back. He left the room and returned with a sheet of paper on which he had written the names and phone numbers of an artist and a smaller print company which, he assured me, would suit me better. Because he was generous enough to tell me I should see the artist before the print company, I was spared making a complete fool of myself a second time.

I called the artist that afternoon (interrupting his nap, I suspected) and asked to see him. He told me to hold on and, in muffled tones, said to his receptionist, who was also his wife, "There's another looney-tune on the phone. Can you get the place cleaned up by tomorrow?" I didn't hear her answer but it must have been affirmative because he came back on the line, saying the only time he could spare would be during his lunch hour the next day.

We made an appointment and I showed up, eager to get my game in the works. When I arrived at the one-room office, which was partitioned into a receptionist/secretary area and a two-drawing-board work area, I was shown past the partition to a man a little older than myself. He was frantically cutting and pasting columns of galleys to art boards. (I learned later, after we had become friends, that it was all faked, designed to impress would-be clients.)

He asked to see my game. Because of the fiasco I had been through the day before, I also gave him what I considered to be a complete list of components. I laid everything out before him, afraid to speak in case I made a fool of myself again. He looked it all over, shaking his head from side to side, letting out a solemn "Hmmm" every now and then. When he finished he looked at me and asked, "Are you sure you want to do this?" I nodded, grinning stupidly. His next question was, "Who do you think will buy it?"

I proceeded to explain my marketing strategy, such as it was, and made an effort to convince him that I not only was serious about doing the game but that I also knew more than he could tell. I must not have been too convincing because the next words out of his mouth were, "Do you have any money?"

Now we were in an area I could handle. "A little," I replied. "How much is all this going to cost?"

Please understand that way back then, longer ago than I care to admit, things were a lot cheaper. "A thousand dollars," responded the man at the drawing board, turning away to hide an irrepressible grin.

"Gee, I don't have anywhere near that," I admitted, pausing for a re- action. Getting none, I stammered, "Gosh, I'm sorry I bothered you. I had no idea it would cost so much. I'm really embarrassed and sorry I wasted so much of your time." I got up and started gathering my ma- terial. At this point, the dialogue really began to roll.

HE: "How much do you have?" (He wasn't about to let this fish off the hook.)

ME: "Well, let's see. After printing and die cutting and making the boxes, I've only got about ... oh, forget it. I'm ashamed to tell you." (I continued to bundle up my items, but slowly.)

HE: "I might be able to do it for less if you give me time to work it in between jobs, but you'll have to leave me alone. Don't be calling me every other day, bugging me. How much do you have?" (He was show- ing more submissiveness than I dared hope.)

ME (with my most sheepish look): "Well, gee, this is embarrassing, I only have about $250."

He looked astonished, hurt, insulted. I shrugged my shoulders and turn- ed to leave. "I'll do it for $500 but you've got to give me four months; no if's, and's or but's," he said, glaring at me through his thick glasses.

That moment, as Bogart once said, was the beginning of a beautiful friendship. This guy turned out to be a heck of an artist. He was fast, dependable, and reasonably priced. He helped produce my first thir- teen games and contributed mightily to their success. For those who are interested, he still is in the Atlanta area, working out of his home and providing professional skills and services to his clients.

Of course, there were drawbacks. He would work all night to meet a deadline but wanted to be sure that I was working all night myself. He could be crabby and cantankerous, or gentle and generous. You never knew until you spoke to him which personality was "on" that day. He had the temperament of an artist, moody and unpredictable, but with that a strong sense of responsibility. We became great friends through- out the years, and to this day he is one of the things I miss most about Atlanta.

Enough old memories. Now back to business!

THE PRINTING PROCESS

The artist you select is going to be your guide and translator in the world of printing. He is going to teach you in depth what I am pro- viding only in passing—an understanding of the terminology you will be hearing. Misunderstanding what people are talking about could cost you money. There is a glossary of printing and art terms at the back of this book, and I suggest you take some time to become famil- iar with them.

Right now we will be sticking to "art talk," although some of it will overlap into printing. As mentioned earlier, the most important piece of art in your game is the box—both top and bottom—sometimes known as the wrap or label. Its job is to persuade prospective buyers to choose your game from among all the others.

There are basically three art mediums for box wraps: a full-color illustration or photograph using the process known as four-color separation; a graphic design of one or more colors accomplished by mechanical separation; and a combination of the two.

Since this is going to be an expensive and important piece of art, spend some time planning and considering the alternatives. You more than likely will wind up using the four-color separation process. It's not cheap but it can be far less expensive than mechanical art which requires a lot of stripping.

Stripping ... Not What
You Think

Stripping is an art involving the skill of craftsmen. A good stripper has the eye of an eagle. He can cut, position, and fasten pieces of film shaped in long strips in such a fashion as to create the most intricate and beautiful color patterns imaginable. Using only the three primary colors (blue, red, yellow) and black (hence the term "four-color process" or "four color printing"), a stripper can work the negatives to create an endless rainbow of colors, shades, and hues. The problem is good strippers are not only hard to find, their skills command a high hourly rate.

Of course, in today's world where technology never stops evolving, computerized machines are replacing not only strippers, but many other aspects of the graphic arts as well. At present the machines are too costly to pose an immediate threat, but by the turn of the century the stripping and separations required for printing jobs will vary, based on the number of special effects rather than the number of colors. For the time being, if your artist tries to talk you into doing an all-mechanical, multi-colored piece of art, make sure he plans on separating the colors mechanically on different overlays.

Back to basics again. The kind of printing involved here is known as "offset." It is called this because a roller picks up ink from the well and transfers it to another roller containing a metal plate which bears the image of what is being printed. This plate, now wet with ink, meets yet another rubber roller and transfers an impression to it. That roller meets a final roller carrying a sheet of paper and imprints the image upon it.

The offset concept supposedly was invented by an Egyptian some time around 2,000 B.C. He made a crude, manual offset press from smooth stones, bees' wax, oil, and ink. In any event, by using this type of printing and four-color process, any picture and virtually any number of colors may be printed. If the printer has a four-color press, one which puts down all four colors as the paper travels through it, the paper is blank when it goes in and finished when it comes out. (Most printers today use five or six color presses and place a coating or varnish on the sheet as it goes through.)

Most people take printing, especially quality printing, for granted. They may make a positive comment when they see a particularly attractive printed piece, without understanding they are seeing an intricate and complex pattern composed of individual dots invisible to the naked eye. These tiny dots, called screens, are the secret of four-color printing. By combining these screens any color can be made from the primary colors and black.

Art for the Box Top   It's important to understand the difference between four-color process separation and mechanical separation. The latter may be done for four-color printing, by hand-stripping and using combinations of dot screens at varying angles with individual camera shots. If the art is simple enough, this method will be cheaper than having a full color separation made. A four-color process separation is done with a camera or, at high-tech operations, with devices employing lasers and computers. If your art is an illustration, photograph or complex, multi-colored design, this will probably be the least expensive way to go. Most likely, the art will be a combination of illustration and type, especially for the game's title.

Now that some of what the artist does makes sense to you let's discuss the type of art to be used for the wrap. Incidentally, the artist whose verbal communication skills come close to matching his artistic talents is a rare bird indeed.

The primary consideration is what will work. This comes back to category and theme. Children's games seem to do well with illustrations or photographs, while adult games are likely to do better with pure graphic designs.

Whether the artist wants to do an illustration, a painting, or a full color drawing, make sure you are comfortable with both his style and his price. Don't be afraid of hurting his feelings on either account. If he goes through with it and winds up producing something completely unacceptable, you still are obligated to pay. You can gauge whether he or she has the ability to get the results you want partly by looking through a portfolio, something all artists have, to show their past works to prospective clients. If you are not able to settle on an illustration or a price, or if you just don't think the artist can deliver the quality you want, it may be time to head back to the library to look for existing photographs or paintings.

TIME FOR MORE LIBRARY RESEARCH   Nearly every library has a collection of magazines. Pore through the ones specifically for photographers, looking for a photo that seems ideal or close to it, for your cover. If you can find one it will probably save you a good bit of money, because the photographer of the picture generally will permit it to be used, for a modest sum, so long as he receives credit (name and address) in the rules of your game. If you cannot come up with anything after going through all the magazines, don't give up. Switch to art prints and art books.

Over the years many thousands of scenes have been painted and preserved in print. Look long enough and you will find a famous, or near famous, piece of art that will work very nicely. This research could be a bonanza for you, for several reasons. If you come up with a picture that is very old, it probably is in the public domain. That means that you can use it legally without having to pay anyone for the right to do so. In this way you may well be able to find an illustration for your game without having to pay an artist $2,000 or more to create it.

While looking through magazines and prints, don't be narrow-minded. Be open to box wraps the images may suggest. Who knows; one of them might offer a better idea than what you had in mind.

**WORKING WITH
THE ARTIST**

Once you have an illustration for the cover and show it to the artist, he or she undoubtedly will find all sorts of things wrong with it. After all, the artist didn't do it or get paid for it. Don't let that bother you. It's understandable, and it comes with the territory.

What you need to do now is to select a type style for the title and subtitle of the game. You want type that suits both the illustration and the game theme. The artist should have pretty much free rein here. With his knowledge of type faces, he should be able to select half a dozen or so from which you can choose. The only other alternative is for you to spend a day or two yourself going through page after page of type books, looking at thousands of type styles.

The next step is to select a background color to border the illustration and wrap around the sides of the box. It should complement the illustration, yet be bright enough to give life to the side panels. After making your choice, decide on a color for the type faces that on both the top and the sides. This color should contrast with the background. The type *must* be clear and easily read. When you have reached a decision, leave the artist alone until he is finished. If he needs you, he'll call.

Sharing this with you reminds me of two experiences I had with box wraps. I was working with the artist I mentioned earlier and the first episode was with the fifth or sixth game I had done. Mike, the artist, always said, "You know enough about printing to be dangerous." I'm afraid this story proves his point. The game was called *SUBMARINE*. I had found this marvelous photograph of a submarine surfacing at night, illuminated by an exploding freighter. It was perfect except for one thing: it was in black and white. By then I knew enough to know the box wrap needed color. Being of Scottish ancestry, I could not resist attempting a two-color mechanical cover to save money.

LISTEN TO THE PRINTER

As I showed Mike a rough sketch alongside the photograph, I suggested he enlarge the photograph to the proper size, cut a mechanical separation on an overlay for the bright area of the explosion, and make the type white. The effect would be an all black box with bold white type and a bright yellow area in the center for contrast and color. (White does not count as a color if the paper is white and is reversed out of an ink.)

Mike felt this wouldn't work, saying he should airbrush (a painting technique) the yellow area and have it separated. Being thrifty, and thinking I knew more than I did, I told him no. I was sure what I proposed would work fine.

Needless to say, it did not. When the job came off the press, parts of the yellow area had blended with the black ink to create a bilious green tinge. It was horrible. But in those days (still the case today, I'm afraid), I did not have all the money in the world and I had to live with it. Fortunately for me, it was a limited print run that sold fairly quickly. Then I managed to sell the game to another company before I had to worry about reprinting.

The second episode had a more pleasing outcome. I think it was my tenth game, one with a science fiction theme. By chance I had seen a color photograph of the Crab Nebula taken by an observatory. It was beautiful, containing subtle shifts of reds, blues, greens, and yellows against a midnight blue, star-filled background. I wrote to the observatory, asking the cost of the negative, with the intention of using the photograph on the box top. Two weeks later I received a four-by-five inch color transparency and a bill for $16. The artist dropped the type into the area occupied by the photo and the box wrap was done. It was simple, gorgeous, and eye-catching.

The point of the first story? Always listen to artists and printers, no matter how much you think you know. Printing is one of those professions plagued with details. It is an industry that is changed constantly by technology. What is true this year may be exactly wrong next. In all the years I have been associated with it, I have yet to meet anyone who knew everything about every aspect of it.

The point of the second story? Sometimes simple is best. Not every box wrap has to be a complicated masterpiece. As long as it fulfills the main objectives of being attractive, attention-getting, and effective in its statement about the game's theme, it could be something as ordinary as a solid blue box. But don't use that. Someone else has already done it; a little hit called *PICTIONARY*.

GAMEBOARD ART

After you have finished the box top, the gameboard is the next item to tackle. Most gameboards are large enough physically and simple enough graphically to be set up for mechanical separations. When four-color process separations are done the charge is basically by the square inch, and a twenty-by-twenty gameboard is a costly number of square inches.

When planning the art for the game board make sure to adhere to the theme. Keep colors complementary to each other as well as to the box wrap and use the same or compatible type faces. In other words, try to retain consistency throughout the art work.

Visual consistency is important to the consumer. When a consumer buys a game he often makes the decision based on how the package looks and the information it contains. If he bought a blue and red box, only to find when he opens the game at home that everything in it is black and gray, he immediately questions his decision and begins thinking negatively about the product. On the other hand, when the game's internal components visually reinforce the consumer's original decision he is relieved, and convinced he made the right choice.

Many first-time game producers are advised to keep their package colorful, so they try to make each component a different and brighter color than the one before. Pretty soon the product winds up looking like a circus. Color is important, but so is pleasing the eye. Stay consistent and the game will look like a well-conceived, quality product. Bounce around with colors and your product will send a message that it is for preschoolers only—not a market limitation you want to impose on your own brainchild.

A few final comments on box and board artwork. Pay strict attention to your finishing touches. For instance, be sure to leave enough tolerance on the box and board artwork. Tolerance is the distance from the edges of the finished art to the edge of the actual box top or game board. Usually one-eighth of an inch is enough. Also—please forgive me if this advice seems unnecessary—take care that the gameboard, when folded, will fit in your box. This is a silly mistake, but I have seen more than one person go crying to their artist when boards and box were delivered and did not fit.

If you are absolutely determined to have an illustration executed by an artist, but are not satisfied with the particular artist you have engaged for graphics, find another one for the illustrations. It is not uncommon for good graphic artists to be poor illustrators, and vice versa. Don't be embarrassed if you have to tell a graphic artist that an illustrator is doing your box wrap art.

THE FINAL WRAP

There are a couple of reasons why the box top and game board were finished first. They make a statement about the game's theme and set a standard or guide for the art to follow. They also take the longest to reach completion as they not only have to be printed but also must be converted into boxes and boards. The last essential item to work on is the box bottom.

The most important aspect of box bottom art is what it says and how it says it. Its sole reason for existing is to make people buy the game. A good way to get a handle on this aspect of selling is go back to the stores and read every box back with a front that grabs your attention. Check to see how many games are displayed so that only one side panel is visible and you will understand the importance of including a line or two of selling copy on these surfaces. Take great care in writing the copy for the box back. If the box top is really good and does its job of getting people to pick up the game, you still are only halfway there. The critical step is convincing people to actually buy the game. It would be a shame if the box back did not fulfill its part of this obligation.

Box Bottom Art

Think of the box bottom as a miniature billboard. When the customer turns the box over, you have four or five seconds to get her attention. If the box is clever and entertaining and gets her interest, you have another twenty seconds or so to sell her. Don't put too much on the box bottom, and especially do not put rules there.

Once the box top art is finished, have the artist determine the image area for the press on which it is to run. If it's not too large and is being printed in process colors, it would not cost too much to have a box back printed at the same time, on the same sheet of paper. If this can be done, you not only will save money for a one-color (black type) box back, for a little extra you also can add some color to the back of the box. Remember that color, anywhere on the box, helps sell.

If the box wrap art image area is too large to allow the back to run at the same time, you are better off sticking with a one-color box back printed on a cheaper grade of paper. It won't look as nice, but the important thing about the back is what it says. You want the best-looking product possible, but when you have a limited budget, this is a good place to save.

While you are testing the box back copy with friends and co-workers, the artist can do the layout and paste-up for the game's other components. This is assuming, of course, that the game has been thoroughly play-tested, the component mix is correct, and the rules are so clear that even a Supreme Court Justice could not misinterpret them. In order to save money and possible embarrassment later, there are a few things the artist should have worked out in advance. In case he did not, I'll go over them here.

THE REST OF THE ART

It's likely your game will make use of one or more decks of cards, game money, play stock certificates, etc. These items can become terribly expensive if they are not handled properly. Try to avoid being charged for any more hand labor than is absolutely necessary.

The printer you have selected should be able to give you exact guidance as to sheet size, card size, and number of cards up for printing to create the most economical product. Experienced printers will also provide clear plastic layouts (often called die vinyls) that show your artist exactly where each piece of work fits on the master sheet.

For instance, if you don't employ a printer with a card collating machine, your customers are not going to find neatly sorted stacks of game money or cards separated into nice little trays when they open the game package. Instead, they'll have a clean-looking sheet of money that has been carefully perforated, for them to tear and sort; or a large folded sheet of cards die-cut and nicked on the edges to hold them in place until the customer punches them out and gathers them into decks.

Five or more years ago this would have been the case for most game makers. Now there are many companies capable of automatically cutting and collating decks of cards or stacks of money, and it is just about as economical as making the customer do it himself. If you are producing a small quantity of games, it's possible you will have to do it the "old-fashioned" way.

"What happened to quality?" you scream. "Is it being thrown out the window?" "My game deserves better!"

Hardly. Many major game companies have adopted this technique for children's games. (Adults demand the quality finish of pre-collated cards.) If you have been doing your homework, you have discovered this. True, some quality is being sacrificed for economy, but this is your first time. Even if unlimited funds are available, you need to keep the cost of the game down to a level where it can be given a competitive, but still profitable, retail price.

Besides, the real quality of a game shows up in how it plays. How it looks is the perceived quality. People buy the game on perceived quality (the box top and bottom and the overall quality of the internal components), but they enjoy it and, more importantly, recommend it to friends on the basis of how it plays.

When I was a kid we did not have a lot of money—like a lot of other kids. Store-bought toys were pretty darn scarce in my house. Even then, the quality of our toys was not that important. The play was the thing! I soon discovered I could use my cheap, opaque marbles to beat the pants off kids who had the fancy, expensive cat's eyes. Point made, I hope.

HOLDING DOWN LABOR COSTS

Hundreds, maybe even thousands of man hours are saved when consumers punch out, gather, and collate the various materials themselves. It really is not all that bad, either ... for younger players. It gives the youngster a feeling of newness to punch out his own parts, as well as something to do for ten minutes while the rules are read. But remember, if you expect your product to compete in the adult game category you have to use the more professional collated card decks.

Back to tolerance. While the art is being done and the cards or money are being pasted down to their respective master sheets, check to make sure there is a one-eighth inch tolerance between the print image areas of each piece. It's cheaper to plan on these tolerance borders being white. An overlay to create a consistent color around the individual pieces can be prepared, but it will cost more because of bleeding.

In graphics jargon the term "bleeding" means simply that a color (or colors) is extended beyond the normal image area, so when the sheet is trimmed the color runs all the way to the edge. Jobs that bleed take more paper than jobs that don't, use more ink (which isn't cheap), and cost a little more to strip and print. In short, try to avoid costly bleeding when making components, but the extra investment may be worth it for your gameboard label.

THE RULES

The art for rules is virtually all type, so there is absolutely no reason to get fancy here. If the length of the rules runs to more than four pages, they probably will have to be saddle-stitched, or stapled on the fold like a thin magazine. That does not cost very much.

With respect to the rules, there are two critically important things to watch. First, be certain to include as many illustrated easy-to-follow examples as are needed. Second, proofread them until you either need new glasses, or a new prescription for your old ones! A couple of bad typographical errors (called typos), or a dropped line in a set of rules, can ruin an otherwise great game and make it fit only for lining the cat's litter box.

Regarding typos ... they breed at night, like unused coat hangers in a closet. I have seen six people proofread a set of rules, get them back after corrections, proofread them again, get them back after more corrections and proofread them a third time, only to find new typos in the last set of corrections. Don't be upset when they're found. Be glad. When proofing something for the third or fourth time, there is a tendency not to really see the type. Force yourself to read one word at a time. *There is no substitute for this.* It is never safe to assume any correction has been made that has not created another, different typo.

Proofreading is difficult, a strain on the eyes, and boring. Your artist will snarl every time you find another error, but it must be done until everything is perfect. It is a good idea to keep one person away from the proofreading until the printer provides you with the final proof. Then, after you have read it for the umpteenth time, give a clean copy to the person who never has seen it before. My last word on this subject is I am absolutely positive there will be a typo on my tombstone (Rest in Piece).

It is impossible to describe every component a game might have, because it depends on the game. Most printed components fall into one of the categories described earlier. For a special piece, such as a wheel with a spinner, or a slide rule type component, make a working prototype. If you are working with one of the few experienced companies that routinely manufactures games they either will be able to produce it themselves or will know someone who can. If you are making your game piece-meal, on your own, take it to the artist on the first trip. If he does not know who can make it locally, take it to some printers and ask them. If you still can't get an answer, alter the component to something that can be produced locally.

As a rule of thumb, if a game requires a custom made piece, have it made locally where a close watch can be kept on its progress. If standard pieces are to be used it is fairly safe to obtain them from whomever you consider to be the best source, regardless of location.

So far we have discussed the artwork, the printed materials for the game. The next step is to discuss other items that are not printed, that must be manufactured in a different manner.

COMPONENTS

In between proofreading sessions, and while the artist is busy finishing the art, try to find sources for the other components. Dice, playing pieces or pawns, colored chips, and marbles are some of the most common pieces that are readily available. You would be surprised at what some manufacturers stock as standard items. If you are looking for something standard, the prices usually are reasonable and shipping dates are good.

Several trade magazines publish annual directories of toy and game manufacturers. You can save time and frustration by obtaining one or more of these directories. You'll find yourself with a "Who's Who" of firms that provide the industry with a full range of services and products. Though none will list every manufacturer in the world, I recommend contacting *PLAYTHINGS* Magazine at Geyer-McAllister Company, 51 Madison Avenue, New York, NY 10010. Their directory seems the most complete. Also check local sources in the Yellow Pages, and ask the printers with whom you are working.

Try to Avoid Customized Components

When you are making low quantities and test marketing, try to stay clear of customized pieces. You can go bankrupt trying to produce them. Injection plastic molds are not cheap. The lowest price I have been quoted recently was $8,000 for a very basic piece, and that was in 1991. Metal pieces tend to have less expensive mold costs, but the per unit cost for producing them will make you sweat blood. Not only that, you have to be very careful about lead content in the pieces or you are likely to be sued, get into trouble with government agencies, and have the game pulled from the market.

If a game requires a special piece that can't be bought or replaced by a standard item, go back to the drawing board to find a way around it. It may be that by printing the necessary image on a sheet laminated to a thick cardboard, and then die-cutting it into whatever shape you need, you will wind up with the same effect for less money. Then, if the game does become a million-dollar seller, you can always go back to the original idea in a reprint. If it can't be made through printing or simple wood turning, you may have to have it manufactured by plastic injection molding.

There are some genuine horror stories involving inexperienced people who decided to handle the production of custom pieces on their own. One of the worst of these concerns a fellow who wanted two vacuum-formed trays to fit in a game box. When delivered they not only did not fit, they wound up costing twice as much as he had been led to expect. He ordered 25,000 sets of these trays, but received only 23,000. When he questioned the manufacturer he was informed they worked on a plus or minus 10% margin and they would not run their machines to produce the difference. This meant the poor fellow could only assemble and sell 23,000 games even though he had paid for components for 25,000. That problem caused him to lose $36,000 in sales—all the potential profits of the venture.

THE LURE OF THE ORIENT

At some point you will discover the economic advantages of having components produced in the Orient. If the quantity is large enough, it's true you will not find a better price anywhere. But *Buyer Beware*. There are more frightening stories being told about oriental production than you would believe. For the most part they have to do with ordering one level of quality and paying by letter of credit; then receiving lesser quality parts, parts of the wrong colors, or nothing at all until three months after the promised delivery date.

A first hand example of this was a client of mine who ordered some customized plastic parts from Hong Kong. The price was better than the best American price by a full 20% and delivery was promised within sixteen weeks, a little longer than the twelve week American schedule. Ten weeks later, during marketing planning, my client called his Hong Kong factory to confirm the arrival dates and was told they might even ship early but not to count on it for advertisement planning.

Armed with that information, the client's marketing and sales forces went to work. They arranged to place full page color ads in a very prestigious and expensive magazine, then informed some select department stores their names would be listed in the ads if they purchased a certain number of games. The plan worked so well that all the targeted sales were made within two weeks. The ads were sent to the magazine and the ad space bill paid. All that remained was to sit back and wait. My client had been clever enough to allow a four week cushion between the date the plastics were supposed to arrive and the date the ads were to appear.

What Went Wrong?

When the week of delivery rolled around the client called Hong Kong to ensure that everything was on schedule. "No problem," he was told by the voice thousands of miles away. "Everything is on schedule."

It wasn't. To make a long story short the items were not produced, let alone shipped, until 20 days before the first ads appeared. Shipping them via surface routing (i.e., ocean freight), the least expensive method, would get them to a U.S. port within a minimum of six weeks. The client had no choice but to air freight the shipment, to hold his orders and maintain credibility with the buyers. His Hong Kong friends told him, "No problem. We have a relative who will ship for half what the airlines charge. Just bring a check to the airport when the goods arrive."

A week later the local airport called and informed my client that his container had arrived and had been processed through customs. He could come pick it up or have it delivered as soon as he brought a check for $18,000 to the office. As it turned out, $18,000 was about nine times the amount budgeted for surface freight. The additional cost was more than enough to make the whole project a losing proposition. My client would have been much better off using a reliable U.S. plastic molder.

Another story comes from one of my competitors. Competitors come in two flavors: those whom you think are the scum of the earth (their mission is to stay in business just long enough to cheat a few dozen customers and muddy up the waters), and those you grudgingly respect for their hard honest work. This particular story is about one of the good guys. While I hated to see it happen to him, there is a lesson to be learned here.

We were competing against each other for a project from a major company. The company wanted turn-key manufacturing; whoever got the job would produce it entirely, including the plastics. This particular game had a lot of plastics; nearly sixty separate pieces. My competitor was awarded the job because he priced the plastics based on having them made in China, where workers sometimes are paid less than five dollars a week. I drank a bottle of Maalox, told my staff we would get the next one, and went on with business.

A few months later, during a meeting with the game publisher who had awarded the contract, he told me there had been a problem. My competitor had manufactured the games and delivered them to the client, shrink wrapped and in cartons — all 200,000 of them. They looked great and were selling well.

Within a few weeks, however, the publisher began receiving customer complaints. Not only were there a lot of plastic parts in the game, some of them fit together to make mechanical devices essential to gameplay. The problem was that when the customers opened the plastic bag containing all the plastics included with each game, they discovered many were missing one or two parts. The publisher immediately conducted a spot inspection, verified that the problem existed, and called my competitor. He had no choice but to remove the shrink wrap from every game, open each game box, open the bag containing plastics, count all the pieces, replace the missing pieces, re-bag the components repack, and shrink-wrap the games. In the context of the size of his business, he lost a fortune.

How Do You Say Caveat Emptor in Chinese?

The lesson is this. Even if you are experienced in this industry it is dangerous to have anything manufactured in the Orient unless you can take the time and have the budget to inspect the product as it is made. So the next time you weigh having something made overseas versus having it produced domestically, remember these two stories — one about an amateur and one about a pro. They both got burned, spent far more than it would have cost to have the product made in the U.S., and learned the value of American business ethics.

Of course, not everyone who deals with Oriental suppliers has these kinds of problems. If you are going to have parts or items manufactured in Hong Kong, Singapore, Taiwan, etc., a good rule to live by is to plan to oversee the process personally, from the time the parts start rolling off the production lines to when they are put on the ship and leave port.

Let your Oriental suppliers know by phone, fax, and letter that you are coming to inspect the process. Before you buy your airline ticket, confirm the start-up dates in writing at least twice. If the Oriental molders know you mean business they are far less likely to alter your delivery schedules or try to use lesser grade materials or poorly molded pieces.

ARRANGING YOUR OWN FINANCING

Now that the creative work is done and you have finished shopping for playing pieces, it's time to get down to the *business* part of the business; to go to the bank, and then to visit a friendly printer. Let's talk about the banker first, since he will provide you with the leverage you will need in your dealings with the printer.

Letter of Credit

When you go to the bank, open either an interest bearing savings account or a short term certificate of deposit that carries only minimal penalties for early withdrawal. Talk to a bank officer and tell him the account has been opened specifically to provide funds for a game project. He might raise an eyebrow, but he will be happy to have the money and even happier you didn't come to see him to borrow the funds for what he probably thinks of as a harebrained scheme. Inform him that you will be calling in the near future for a letter of credit, payable to a printer upon your authorization.

The strategy behind securing a letter of credit is two-fold. Let's say you own a local company which will stake the game project. Unless it has an impeccable credit rating—impressive enough to convince the printer to bill you for the work—the printer will want a good portion, if not all, of his payment up front. I'm not saying he's wrong. I have been in this business long enough to have seen many printers who didn't cover themselves end up eating a huge unpaid bill.

It may be the first time you have produced a game, but it is almost certain the printer has had a number of undercapitalized people approach him with a game that was a "guaranteed" best-seller. In short, a printer who has any sense, who does not know you from Adam, simply is not going to get involved in a project without financial security. Why should he? He would be the one taking all the risks!

The second reason for opening the bank account is so that you can provide yourself with some protection. By using the letter of credit form of payment, the printer is guaranteed his money when the job is delivered, and you are guaranteed the printer is not going to take half of the money in advance and then proceed to produce the game at his own "whenever I can work it in" pace. The letter of credit also establishes your credibility with the printer. When he sees the LC, he will know you are serious. He will quote or estimate the cost of the job more quickly, as well as being more willing to work with you to get the best job done at the best price.

VENTURE CAPITAL

I have assumed you have the money to produce your own game; if not in ready cash, at least enough real assets to provide collateral for a loan. What if you don't? You almost certainly will not get an unsecured loan from a banker. So, where do you get it?

You probably will be relieved to know that most people do not have the funds to produce and market their own projects. The money to market games is often more important than money for production, and it has to be raised somewhere. Friends and relatives often can be enticed into becoming investors, but this is risky and really should be your last resort. Chances are the friendship or family will split up over the project whether it succeeds or fails. If you decide not to test those personal relationships, give the world of venture capitalism a try and you very quickly will learn the real value of money.

Venture capitalists are groups or individuals who have money; enough that they are able to invest in more normal business activities and still have a little left over to try some "off the wall" idea that might make them even richer. They usually do not have any desire to work in the companies in which they invest, but they often demand a substantial (sometimes a controlling) interest in those companies.

How much control will they expect? Since venture capitalists know they are your last hope they tend to be demanding. If a project looks as though it has genuine potential and—even more important—if they are impressed by the people behind the project, you will have captured their attention ... but not yet their money. If they are going to back you, they will insist on a substantial chunk of the project.

When he computes how much of the profits the inventor is to keep, the venture capitalist normally will ask to see documentation of the amount of actual money spent to date (the inventor's investment of "sweat equity" up to this point has no bearing). Take the proven cash outlay, multiply it by 1.5, then figure the results as a percentage of the amount of the venture capitalist's investment. For example, if the inventor had a cash outlay of $10,000, multiplying that amount by 1.5 gives you $15,000. If the capitalist is asked to put up $100,000, then the inventor would be allowed to keep 15% of the business.

Seems almost confiscatory, doesn't it? Not every deal is so hard but the above example is not unusual.

How to Find *Venturesome* Venture Capitalists

It's not as difficult as you might think. The first step in the process is to ask around. Investors in stocks, bonds, and real estate often are approached by venture capital brokers; i.e., people who try to match individuals with ideas with those who have money. You may even find a venture capitalist or a broker simply by asking friends or relatives.

Newspaper and financial magazine classified ads often have sections listing names of people seeking investors and those looking to invest. Making the right connection may be as simple as buying a few Sunday papers.

The reference department of your local library also can prove very helpful in your search. It contains directories that classify types of businesses by county and city, within each state. Venture capital firms and bankers are everywhere. Finding them isn't really the hard part, but getting them to say "yes"—*that's* the hard part.

One shark to be wary of is the venture capital broker. For a large fee, this character will put you in the same room with an interested party who supposedly has enough money to finance your project. The catch is you will not be told anything about the money connection before the meeting, but you will have to pay the fee in advance; no refunds, no guarantees, thank you very much. I often have wondered just who is put in the room with you. Do people pay thousands of dollars to make a presentation to the broker's brother-in-law?

THE BUSINESS PLAN

The business plan, or prospectus, is one of your most essential tools for attracting investors. Because of its importance, it must be professional and highly informative.

Putting together a good business plan is not easy. There are people who make their livings writing such plans and they are paid handsomely for doing so. Once you try your hand at it, you will understand why. It's a lot of work.

Before getting down to the job of writing you should look at a completed plan of good quality. When you are in your library's reference department, look for books on how to write business proposals. Reading one or two will go a long way toward helping you create a successful plan.

After doing some research on the subject you still have a tremendous amount of pre-writing preparation to do. From both the inventor's and investor's points of view, the two most important issues requiring your full and careful attention are marketing and management.

Emphasis on Marketing and Management

The marketing section of your proposal should detail the following: how the product will be sold and to whom; who will be doing the selling; when the selling and buying will take place; when and where the ads and promotions will appear, and how much they will cost. In short, you need to create a real plan, one that is businesslike and attainable.

I have a friend who is an investment banker, a venture capitalist. He once said there are three kinds of business plans. The first kind (80% are in this category) is put together to raise money, then tossed in the trash bin when the money has been obtained. 15% are prepared as a formality, to raise money that is already available. Only 5% are used not only to raise money, they also are real business plans, full of strategies and tactics, outlines and guides, benchmarks and jumping-off points—in other words, all the elements needed to put and keep a business on course. That's the kind of plan you want to put together.

The management team is your second important consideration. Potential investors want to be assured the people running the new company's day-to-day activities have the talent, ability, expertise, and determination necessary to provide an excellent chance for success. Never offer to work for the company for nothing the first few years. The idea does not make any sense, and investors do not expect it. If the investors are interested they will expect to pay a reasonable salary to those behind the idea.

The management section of the plan also should include the names of the specific consultants or firms who likely will be contracted in some capacity. For example, you will be using graphic artists, printers, plastics manufacturers, and maybe even some marketing and advertising consultants. All these people should be mentioned in your list of involved parties.

Business Plans and Raising Money

Larry Blackwell is a friend and partner in the game business. Larry worked in corporate finance for many years before getting into the game business by self-publishing a mass-market game. In his corporate finance role, he evaluated hundreds of business plans and the companies behind them. Mr. Blackwell is a partner in Game Plan, Inc., a product development and licensing firm specializing in toys and games. Wanting to take advantage of his expertise (and our friendship), I asked him to talk about the benefits of a well-executed business plan and what sets it apart from most business plans.

The serious reader is advised to have a fresh highlighter before reading this section.

A SEMINAR IN BUSINESS PLANS AND RAISING MONEY

Okay, so you like what you have read so far and you want to self-publish your game. Which of the following should you *not* do until later? (Feel free to choose more than one.)

1. Call your best friend and tell him or her you have decided to self-publish your game.

2. Call the bank to arrange an appointment with a loan officer.

3. Write a business plan.

4. Manufacture your game in a small run and start selling it.

5. Call your wealthy brother-in-law and tell him what an investment opportunity you have for him.

The correct answers are numbers 1, 2, 4 and 5. An important reason for not doing them is that all four commit you to a venture you still don't know a great deal about, unless you have done it before. The business plan is your thorough evaluation of the business venture and your guidebook towards the business' objectives. Even so, many entrepreneurs come up with excuses for not writing a plan.

Reasons Why You Do Not Need a Business Plan

What would be your excuse for not writing a business plan? Perhaps you don't need a plan since you are just bringing a game to market (after all, it's not rocket science, right?). Maybe you don't need to put your plan on paper; it's in your head. Maybe you don't have time since starting the business now — getting moving before someone steals your idea or beats you to the market—is much more important.

Possibly you just can not bring yourself to do it, or feel you are not qualified or capable of doing it. Perhaps you think it doesn't serve much useful purpose after it helps you raise the money. Maybe you don't need to raise money since you can fund it yourself, so why bother with a business plan. However appealing or valid these excuses may appear, they are all just excuses; foolish rationalizations that satisfy our conscience and tell us it is okay to go ahead anyway.

There are four main reasons why entrepreneurs trying to start businesses do not write good, solid business plans. By the end of this chapter, only three of them could apply to you. The four reasons are ignorance, impatience, arrogance, and laziness. It's blunt, but true. But getting entrepreneurs to write good business plans can be more difficult than talking someone into drilling his own root canal without benefit of anesthesia.

Just How Important Is It?

It would be impossible to overdramatize the importance of writing a thorough business plan. For starters, it may demonstrate to you that the business as planned will not work. Or it may work, but it will not bring you the rewards you are seeking. You may decide the business is sufficiently different from what you expected before you began to write the plan that you no longer are interested. You may discover you need more money than originally thought; or maybe less money. You will almost always find ways to save money, to improve productivity, and get more for your money when you write a good business plan.

Sure it takes time, and yes it requires discipline for someone anxious to start seeing some visible progress. It's even hard work. But would you build a 7,000 sq. ft. house by laying the foundation, ordering some wood, bricks, and mortar, and *then* sit back and decide what kind of house you wanted and what it should look like? It's no different with a business. Why do anything until you have a plan for running the business? Making changes on paper is infinitely easier and less expensive than changing an ongoing business (assuming the business is still *in* business).

When you sit down to write a good, solid business plan, you should have two goals:

1. To conduct an honest assessment of the business, and your role in it.

2. To provide a plan for guidance toward your stated objectives, and the means of evaluating your progress.

Notice neither goal was to raise money. By working to achieve the first goal, you will find honest answers to such questions as: "Is it really probable the business will bring me the rewards I'm seeking? Would my role in the business make me happy, even if the business were only breaking even for several years? Is the lifestyle for me? Are my expectations realistic?"

Remember, it is much easier to start a business than to get rid of one, even if you are successful. Issues addressed by achieving the second goal include: "What is our definition of success? How much money can we make or lose? What are our risks? Which parts of the business are the most critical? When and how much financing will be needed? How do we achieve our business objectives? How are we doing? How do we reward our people for their successes?"

By achieving these two goals, you will have answers for situations which would plague or destroy your business otherwise. You also will have a guide plan for your company as you grow; both a means of navigating and a point toward which to navigate.

Several factors could get in the way of achieving these business plan goals: dreaming of the money you will make, and writing the plan only for the purpose of raising money. Every time you dream of the money you are going to make or tell yourself the plan is really just to satisfy someone else, you are denying yourself the opportunity to uncover a flaw or make an improvement in your original plan. Achieve these goals by playing a game. The game is to discover as many flaws and potential improvements in your original plan as possible. The more you discover, the closer you are to reaching your goals of honest assessment and eventual success.

Putting the Business Plan Together

When you make the decision to put together a business plan, some of you will ask if you should do it yourself or hire someone to do it for you. I strongly recommend you write the plan yourself. Even if you have to hire someone to guide and assist you, you will benefit immensely by going through the steps of writing a solid plan. Hiring someone to do it all may be easier, but you will be cheating yourself. The plan needs to be the product of your thoughts and insights. You can't fully achieve the goals of writing a plan unless you do it yourself.

It is time to clarify one point. *Using* your business plan to raise money is not a sin. In fact, it's smart. The sin is *writing* the plan for that purpose. If you intend to use your business plan to raise money, your business plan must look professional. With typesetting software available for every personal computer, there is no reason to hand someone a business plan that looks mediocre. The readers of your plan, savvy investors and your employees alike, are human. Human beings tend to assign credibility to documents that look professional. (Professional investors will deny this, but it's true.) Fancy bindings will not make it look professional, but a thoughtful well-designed and produced presentation of the information will.

Also for those of you who will use your plan to raise money, a secondary goal of the two goals outlined earlier is to build credibility with your potential investors. Investors are investing in management, not a product. Products don't manufacture, distribute and sell themselves. Management is the key to a business' success or failure. Your plan must instill in your potential investors a certain comfort level with respect to your ability and judgment. The best way to do that is to be credible in person and through your plan. If you try to fluff your way through your plan, investors will not—and should not—give you the time of day.

Be prepared to do a great deal of research. Don't be bashful. Call people. Be creative in your resourcefulness. As you put together the plan, think in terms of running a game company, not creating and selling a single game. It will help you focus your energies on systems, not a single product.

A business plan may be anything from a five page outline of functional goals and summaries of methods for attaining those goals, to a 40-60 page detailed blueprint. Probably somewhere between the two is what you need; a plan in the 8-15 page range. Your plan should include goals, strategies, and methods of implementation and reward for each of the functional areas and for the company as a whole. The business plan outline below lists more detail than you may have, but it is provided for those who want to include or consider more information rather than less. The main sections of any business plan are:

Business Plan Summary

The summary is a brief description of your business or the challenges, the risks, and the potential rewards. Mention your competitive advantages and why you believe you will achieve your objectives. If you need money, mention the amount needed and in what form (a loan or purchase of stock), and how investors will get their money back. The summary should be as upbeat as credibility allows (with appropriate attention given to the risks), and no longer than two pages, preferably one.

Description of the Company

The company description should be a single page detailing the form of company (limited partnership, sole proprietorship, corporation, or Sub S corporation, etc.), the initial capitalization, the location of the company, and the principal contact person. If your company has been in business, expand the description to include the number of employees, a summary of current and past sales and income, a history of your business' progress, and how it differentiates itself in the market.

Products and Services

This will include a detailed description of the games (products or services) you are bringing to the market, and why consumers need or will want them. Describe what differentiates them from other products or services currently available.

Management

This should provide a detailed description of the management positions and organizational structure, the persons occupying those positions, their experience and achievements, why they are uniquely suited to achieve the company's goals, their goals for their positions, and how they will be compensated and measured for both salary and incentive bonuses. Put a modest salary in for yourself, since investors will not expect you to work full-time for nothing. Remember, investors and your employees alike are investing in you and the company's management, so give this section considerable thought.

Competition and Risk Factors

This section discusses your competitors and their products and services, why they are currently successful (what need they are fulfilling), what their Achilles' heel is, the barriers to entry within your industry, and the unique risks in your business and industry. In games, a unique risk would be that your major asset, the game on which you spend a great deal of money to develop, may be worthless or become worthless sooner than expected.

Marketing Plan

Here you outline the plan which details how you will distribute your product and create demand for it at both the wholesale and retail levels. Answer questions such as what kinds of salespeople you will use, how they will be compensated, the geographic area on which you will focus, promotional and advertising budgets, ad and promotional media to be used and why those media (e.g., radio and magazines) are best suited for your products and services, what your marketing goals are and how you will measure your progress, how you will implement your marketing strategies and take advantage of the things which differentiate your game or company. Include timetables, trade shows you plan to attend, etc.

Manufacturing and Operations

A detailed discussion of how you will manufacture your game or have it manufactured, special factors to be considered, advantages and risks of your chosen method, systems for product development, fulfilling orders, invoicing, delinquent accounts and estimated default rate, etc.

Financial Plan and Pro-Forma Financial Statements

Detailed financial statements of past performance, if any, and projected (pro-forma) performance for the next twelve months and the following two years. Include a discussion of past performance or major assumptions used in developing the pro-forma statements. The statements include Balance Sheet, Income Statement, and Cash Flow.

The financial section gets more entrepreneurs in trouble than any other section in the business plan. Many projections are so fanciful that investors stop reading. On the other hand, some do not provide adequate return for the investors or for the business itself. This might not be the fault of the business plan, but it may raise the question as to why anyone is pursuing this business.

Take the time to do your homework. Find out what a reasonable return is for your industry and type of product, and know what your competitors' ratios are. Your projected results should differ only because of what you can support through solid reasoning, not hopes. Be sure you understand the difference between an income statement and a cash flow statement. In the short term, your business will survive on cash flow, not income. Your projections should show when cash will be needed and how it will be used.

Finally, build your projections on an integrated balance sheet, income statement, and cash flow computer model. I build them on spreadsheets because only spreadsheets have the flexibility I desire. Make every assumption easily changeable. The projections you build on a spreadsheet or similar software will allow you to project your cash needs, available cash, and an array of other items based on constantly changing conditions. And trust me; the conditions will change, constantly.

If you are unable to develop the model yourself, hire someone who can build it for you, based on your input as to what the financial relationships and assumptions are. If you hire someone to write your pro-forma statements from a word processor or in any other unchangeable format, you might as well take that money and buy a painting with it. It's certainly will be a useful, and you'll enjoy the painting—which is more than you can say for hard-typed numbers. Hard-typed projections are a waste of time and paper.

Appendices Include résumés of management, market research summaries, or other pertinent data not appropriate for other sections. In short, inclusions here should be optional reading for those who are truly interested. Hint: Don't rely on market studies to persuade readers. It is difficult to evaluate a study's true validity.

Turn-Ons and Turn-Offs If the major goals of a business plan are to provide an honest assessment of the business and to provide guidance for the business, then it goes without saying you have to be honest with yourself as you are writing the plan. But since many people write plans with the goal of raising money, they lose sight of the need to be honest and credible, and to gather a thorough understanding of the business.

Based on my experience in reviewing and writing business plans, I have developed a list of elements in a business plan which lessen or destroy the credibility of management.

TURN-OFFS • Discussing matters (e.g., about the industry and competition) about which you know less than the reader. If you don't know it well, do not discuss it. General industry figures can be misleading to the uninitiated, so talk to people in the know before relying on something you read.

• Financial statements projected beyond three years. I saw a business plan which projected how much toilet paper the company would use five years later. Yes, I'm exaggerating a little, but be realistic; we really don't know much about what will happen 18 months from now, much less five years from now. You should not take seriously projections for your new venture beyond three years. Why expect anyone else to?

• Numbers projected with cents (two decimal places). A pet peeve, albeit a humorous one, for people who read projections. Are the writers of these numbers really serious?

• Income, sales, and other line items far exceed normal projections. Several companies, such as RMA and Standard & Poor, publish industry norm studies. These are available at your local library. If your ratios are far out of norm and are unsupported, your plan will look like a pipe dream to anyone reading it.

• Key assumptions are unexplained or are insupportable. At best, it will appear as though you have not thought it through. Or as above (even worse), as though the plan is not grounded in reality.

• Fluff. A thick report with little meat. Form has triumphed over substance. You would not believe how many business plans are guilty of this. Don't kid yourself: almost anybody can spot it. Enthusiasm is fine, but include enough meat to feed the hungry.

• Too much emphasis on product. This will be difficult for you to avoid, since your business will be introducing a new game to the market. But from the investor's standpoint, you could be selling widgets, (very popular widgets, everyone hopes). However, the widgets will not sell themselves. They must be manufactured, financed, distributed, and marketed. Emphasize the management and systems which will make your company successful.

• Unrealistic expectations. They contribute to the pipe dream look, not where most investors want to put their money.

• No provision for investors getting their money and profits out. From an investor's standpoint, money is not really made until it's back in his hands—profit included. If you don't indicate how investors will get their money back, why should they think you care about their welfare or investment?

• Inadequate investor reward for the risks taken. Just as you think your idea is the most valuable part of your business, investors tend to think their money is a valuable asset and they want to be compensated fairly for the risks they are taking. While investing in you or your idea may not seem like much of a risk to you, investors see it as an entirely different matter. They don't know you, their money is already earning a reasonable return with very little risk, and they have seen lots of great ideas flop (really). If their potential return is not sufficient, they will go to the next business plan.

For a new game from a new company, it's truly difficult to tell you what a minimum sufficient return is. Perhaps it will provide a guideline to say I could not recommend investors take the risks for an anticipated annual return of less than quadruple the prime rate; probably more. Venture capitalists typically look for an anticipated annual return of 40% and higher. Naturally, they do not get that from every investment. Many of their investments produce little return or produce losses, so they must compensate for them with a few very profitable investments.

• Management with little or no experience in the applicable field(s). As stated earlier, investors are investing in management, not in a product or service. If you can't get people with experience, hire a consultant who knows the ropes to be your advisor and learn from him. Good consultants can save you much money and heartache. You may trumpet their accomplishments in your plan, but don't let that be the only reason you hire them.

• Projections for income statements and balance sheets only, not cash flow. Cash flow is the lifeblood of any business. Not to include cash flow projections is to demonstrate the writer of the plan does not understand the importance of cash flow.

• No idea of how much money is really needed to finance the venture. If you have not done your homework and projected your cash needs, how can you expect investors to believe you can run a business?

• Projections not in a computer format (spreadsheet or something else equally flexible). If I find out the projections provided came from an inflexible format (word processor, typewriter, etc.), I know the numbers are mere window dressing. They can't be used a month later, they can't be used for sensitivity testing, and they can't be used to provide answers. The real purpose of the projections is to provide answers, not icing for a cake.

TURN-ONS • Good, solid management with a good track record in the applicable fields. Not always possible for a low budget start-up, but aim for it. Personally, I admire management who have scrapped and done well with very little.

• Realistic numbers (ratios either in the norm or with well-supported reasons for being out of the norm.) Assumptions are clearly disclosed and supported with solid reasoning. Numbers can be easily modified to answer "what if's."

• Provision for investors getting their money out. Indicates management understands the needs of investors and has thought through the plan. Shows investors how they will get their investment back and their profit out, either through dividends, distributions, sale of the company, etc.

• A thorough understanding of the industry, the business, and your business' competitive advantages and disadvantages. Demonstrates you know which areas of the business are the most critical or sensitive. This instills confidence in management's ability to reach goals and to react to changes as they occur.

• No fluff and little hyperbole. Five pages is better than 35 pages *if* you have covered everything in the five pages. Don't write for length, write for content. It is exciting to read a business plan that cuts to the core of the issues right away.

Raising Money with Your Business Plan

Now you have finished your business plan and have decided to pursue the business, but you need a little money. Let's talk about how you might get that money.

Having self-published and licensed games myself, I can share with you a few thoughts specific to the game industry.

• Don't take on debt to launch your game. Raise equity (stock) capital **only**. Do not mortgage your house or your pets. If you do, there is a "better than you think" chance that you not only will see your games sitting in your garage, but that your garage will be attached to the house being hauled away with your pets inside. (The bank will not want your kids since it does not want to feed them and can't resell them.)

Here is a secret regarding debt. When you are spending borrowed money, you must be able to buy at least a dollar of assets for every dollar spent. We are talking real assets here, not an inventory in a warehouse. You cannot do that in the game business with any certainty.

• Do not raise money from family or friends. Most people do this because they have not made this particular mistake before and because it's easy compared to convincing strangers to part with their money. If you are willing to part with your family and close friends, ignore this paragraph. The risks are so high in the game business, you should really think twice before involving people who are close to you. Even if your venture is successful, this kind of financing usually is regretted later.

• Consider raising money in two stages; one to prove the appeal and marketability of the game, the second to provide for distribution and promotion. Since not every game will make it to the second stage, it will be much cheaper for everyone involved. If you still decide to do everything at once, consider introducing your game regionally to lower your costs and to refine your marketing approach before going national.

Other Considerations

There are a few other steps you might want to take which are not specific to the game industry but are true for most new ventures.

• Protect yourself by organizing your business as a Sub-S corporation. A tax attorney can describe the benefits and restrictions.

• Conduct a thorough self-assessment one last time before starting your business. If the pursuit of money is your main motivation, think twice. You will have a business, but the money may not come.

• Get your financial systems in place before your product is finished. Starting sales or production without having your financial systems in place is an invitation for disaster. Cash flow will be untrackable, and costs can get out of control. At the least, opportunities will be missed. When the business gets going, it's difficult to find time to set up your financial systems. Do it early.

• Decide how much control you are willing to surrender. If most of the money for your game company is going to come from outside sources, it is likely you will end up with a minority stock position; less than 50%, ensuring you will lose absolute control. With less than absolute control, it means your investors theoretically could remove you from any office in the company. If that is completely unacceptable to you, do some creative thinking on how you could structure the financing and still retain control. It is not always possible, but it is worth a try.

• The list of potential investors is limited only by your imagination. Anyone with cash is a potential investor. Since you do not want to get money from friends and/or family, a good source of investors to consider, for a new game from a new company, would be people within the game industry. They know the potential risks and rewards, and can also provide valuable advice and contacts. Sources of professional investors are various venture capital firms. They invest their own money as well as money from institutions and private individuals in smaller start-up and early stage companies. You can find a list of them at your local library. Be reminded that venture capitalists have a reputation for being demanding investors.

• Prior to making your pitch, talk to someone familiar with securities law to make sure your efforts to raise money are completely legal. It is easier to run afoul of these laws than you might think.

• Before you meet with potential investors, be sure you know your business plan inside out. If you have had help from professionals, make sure you *understand* what you know. Practice your presentation with a friend or employee playing devil's advocate. The more diligent investors will try to find weaknesses in your plan. There is no reason to be offended; they are just trying to protect their money.

The presentation is simply an education under fire. Be yourself. If you are successful in getting financing, you will be seeing a lot of your investors. It helps to take people such as key employees, committed investors, or consultants with you to your meeting, both for your comfort and the investors'. In your meeting focus on management first, then the product. Use visual aids for clarification and image building. Tell the investors how you will make them money. If you completely understand the venture, you will impress the investors. That does not necessarily translate into money. It simply means they might read your business plan. Give them copies of your plan, and tell them you are available for questions at any time.

• As you get rejections from one investor after another, understand that they are looking for investment opportunities that meet particular criteria. No game may satisfy those criteria. Don't take their rejection to mean your game or business is flawed. On the other hand, listen to their specific feedback; learn from it, and use it to your benefit.

• To hear their rejections—and maybe a yes—you probably will have to pursue them by telephone. Follow up. Some investors may be testing your determination. Each rejection gets you that much closer to a yes. It is a game of odds. With hard work and a little luck, you may get your financing.

LIFE AFTER RAISING MONEY

After using it to raise money, most entrepreneurs put their business plan on a shelf. However, if the plan was properly written, you will not want to put it on your shelf. It will be your guidebook. It will contain real goals and objectives, systems for rewarding the attainment of those objectives, strategies and tactics, methods of implementation, and it will be flexible enough to change as conditions warrant.

Do not allow your business plan to become stale. Rerun your projections and update your plan periodically. Involve as many of your employees as possible in the update. Have them write sections of the plan, or better yet, have them write one sentence objectives as an abbreviated, goal-oriented outline of your plan. A well designed and executed business plan must not be shelved. It's more than a book ... *it's a plan.*

POSTSCRIPT: HOW MUCH MONEY ARE WE TALKING ABOUT?

People always want to know, "How much money do I need to launch my game?" Your business plan will give you the best answer, but I will supply some round figures for those of you who are just curious at this point; not quite ready for self-publishing a game. The following figures include money for minimal inventory but not for product development, and actual numbers will vary dramatically based on the game, the amount spent on marketing, and other considerations.

For a very small, local launch, think in terms of a minimum of $25,000. A large, local launch will require at least $75,000. A regional introduction can go through $150,000 and more. To launch a game nationally requires $400,000 just to hit the high spots, with many, many areas left uncovered. In contrast with these numbers, large game manufacturers spend $1,200,000 and more to launch a new game nationwide, and they don't have to spend a penny to develop their distribution systems—a costly situation for a start-up company.

You can see why I partnered so quickly with this young man.

Now that you are armed with the business plan, the next step in raising money is the presentation.

THE PRESENTATION

At times I have been hired to take part in presentations to groups of venture capitalists. I call these little get-togethers "shark feeds," and would not attend one without being paid, and paid well. Sometimes these are bearable, almost pleasant events, but more often they are grueling sessions with the potential investors behind the bright lights and you under them.

When you participate in one of these meetings make sure you know your business plan inside out and be prepared to back up every statistic in it. If there is a flaw in the plan, these guys will find it. That's their job, so try not to become defensive if the questions get petty. Often they are just trying to prove they know as much about the business plan as you do.

It also is an excellent idea not to face these financial wild cards alone. Bring as many of your experts as will come, for the more people you produce to demonstrate interest in the project, the more credible it will appear.

Just be yourself at the meeting. Let your potential partners see the *real* you. If they choose to invest, you will be seeing a good bit of each other, so you should establish an honest, open relationship from the very beginning. Speculator investors tend to be very sharp people. You are not about to fool them, so act natural. If things go right you will get your financial backing and you'll be ready to start your business.

The next step will be to go see some printers. Since a number already have been contacted and your artwork produced to fit their standard sizes, the list should not take too long to complete.

VISITING THE PRINTERS

Printers are just like other businessmen. They range from scam artists (and worse) to those whom God Himself would hire to print His brochures ... if He had any. The artist you select probably will be able to recommend one or more printers to you, and one of these might be right for the project. But remember the graphic arts business can be an "I'll scratch your back if you scratch mine" business, just like any other. The odds are the recommended printer will be a good one, capable of working effectively with your artist, but be careful; there are many capable printers who don't know anything about taking a game from start to finish. Don't rely only on your artist's recommendations. Make some inquiries yourself. Satisfy yourself that the printer selected can do the job. After all, it's your game—and your money.

If you dig hard enough and are successful in locating a printer who makes games, ask to see a representative selection of games the printer has produced in the last two years. If the printer does in fact manufacture games on a regular basis he should have no problem showing you a dozen or so samples. If the printer shows you one or two games you have never heard of, that can't be found in any retail store, and then tries to show you what a wonderful job he does for his huge corporate clients, don't be impressed. Commercial printing is totally different from producing games. For one thing there usually is a higher markup. If the printer does show you samples of a number of games from the last two years, ask for a list of clients for whom he made them. Tell the printer you would like to check his references. If he is good he won't mind, and it will help put your mind at ease.

After getting recommendations and checking them out carefully, narrow down your list of potential printers to three or so. Call them and ask to speak to a salesperson. More than likely you will have to leave a message and wait for someone to return your call. This is a good sign. It means the company's sales people are out selling, which means the company is busy, which usually means the company is a good one.

When the salesperson calls back, tell him about your project. Inform him that the final artwork is ready to be completed and that you would like to make an appointment to see him at his office. This last part is important. You are going to be spending a lot of money and you deserve a chance to see the plant where the work will be done. If the salesman says it would be more convenient for him to come to you, tell him to pick another time as you really would like to see his operation. If the salesperson still persists in visiting you instead, tell him you have to go and call the next name on your list. Don't start out by dealing with someone who is either ashamed of his plant or who really is a printing broker with no plant of his own.

Be Fully Prepared   Bring all your component specifications with you to these appointments. In addition, have your itemized list of components with you for reference, so that you can quickly tick off such requirements as: the number and size of each part; the number of colors involved; instructions on bleeding; the type of paper to be used and the finish on it (whether trimmed, die-cut, folded, or perforated).

Bringing a full prototype is a good idea. Impress upon these people the fact that you know your game thoroughly and demonstrate your seriousness about this project. Let them have the freedom to suggest changes in sizes, numbers of colors, numbers of cards in decks, etc. They are not trying to redesign your game, just trying to design the components so they can be produced with maximum efficiency on their equipment.

Regardless of how much you have learned so far, there is a good chance some questions will be asked you won't understand. Don't worry about it. Use these questions to educate yourself. Ask for explanations in laymen's terms. It's amazing how some printing salespeople warm up to explaining their craft if someone is genuinely interested. If the conversation is still beyond your understanding, simply ask to see samples of what is being described.

Don't Talk Money ... Yet   At several points during these interviews you will be tempted to turn the conversation to the subject of money. Don't! Any figure at this point would be meaningless. Estimates involve much more than guesswork—for your sake and the printer's. They are exacting and tedious to do, and always take at least a few days. To help keep the cost as low as possible, emphasize the flexibility of the game's components and identify the sizes of those that can be made smaller in order to allow them to be ganged with one another.

The Importance of Ganging   Ganging simply means printing on the same sheet two or more jobs that share common colors and paper stock. For example, a game may utilize two different decks of cards. They may be of different sizes and have different images printed on their fronts and backs but if they are printed by four-color process on the same type of paper, and are the right size to fit the printer's press, they can be combined into one set of negatives, plates, and press run. This will save you a considerable amount of money compared to printing them all as separate items.

It could be particularly worthwhile to gang the labels. The box top and gameboard labels are usually printed on the same paper with the same colors. If the printer's press size will allow it and if you can make the game work with a slightly smaller size you may be able to gang the box top and gameboard label *and* the box bottom, a spinner, and card box top labels all on one sheet. What this means, especially for short print runs, is that you will only be paying for one set of plates, one make-ready, and one run through the press.

Make sure people understand you know about ganging and want the printer to do so wherever possible. The more ganging, the more money saved. In some cases a printer may try to talk you out of this. When ganging two or more four-color illustrations on the same sheet, for instance, a certain amount of color accuracy may be lost because the correction of one color while the job is on the press tends to throw off another color. If the printer mentions this, it's not necessarily because he is trying to get more money. Rather, it's because he cannot tell how critical you are going to be about the final job. That's something we should discuss at this point.

Quality: What Is it Worth to You?

I work with a company that prints everything from cheap, one-color placemats for fast food restaurants to limited edition, fine art prints sold through galleries for hundreds of dollars. The difference in quality between these two extremes is enormous. The fine art prints have to be perfect, every hue an exact match to the original. The placemats, on the other hand, have a limited purpose. They are to be used and discarded. The purchasers of the placemats see no reason to pay extra to insure that each one is exactly the same as the next.

Next time you are in a restaurant, take note of several placemats. You won't be able to tell the difference between them because you will be seeing only a few at a time. They will look good for what they are. If you saw thousands of them at the same time they would still look good but you would be able to spot slight variations in color. Some would be darker than others and so forth.

My point is a game is going to fall somewhere between these two extremes; not a fine art print, but not a placemat either. You won't want the printing to be so poor that no two box wraps look the same. On the other hand, you won't need and should not pay for the exact repetition of a limited edition print. Games are not framed and hung or scrutinized intently. They are kept in closets and taken out occasionally to be played. Once the customer has removed the shrink wrap, the box is going to become soiled and scratched. So, if there is more than one piece of four-color printing that can be ganged, inform the printer you are aware of the problems with color correction but are not overly concerned with perfect matches. You just want the job to look good and the colors to be consistent.

Now It's Time to Talk Money

While you are itching to ask how much everything is going to cost, the printer is trying to figure out the most tactful way to bring up the subject of money. He typically will want at least half in advance (when he is actually ready to begin the work), with the balance payable on delivery.

There normally is no charge for estimating a commercial printing job, but if a particular printer routinely does game projects, he may charge a fee to cover the cost of his estimate. Most people are as ignorant of the costs involved in making their game as they are of the amount of work that goes into creating accurate estimates. When they are told what it will cost to manufacture their game and informed the printer will not extend them credit they usually beat a hasty retreat. In that situation, the printer is out the salary of one or more estimators for two or three days.

If the printer has a reputation for making games he is likely to get several requests daily for estimates. If he did not cover himself he would be paying an estimator to spend all his time quoting projects that never got printed. Consequently, to save himself money and to weed out those who are casually curious, he charges a fee to cover the cost of his estimator's time. Eventually that amount is applied toward the total bill, if and when he gets the printing job. Don't be suspicious of these fees, or resent them. It probably means the printer knows what he is doing and has enough expertise to save you a lot of time, frustration, and money later on.

A Turnkey Job—or Piecemeal?

Exactly what is the printer going to do for you? The answer is as much as you want done and as much as you are willing to pay for. Some printers, but not many, will do a game from start to finish, including the art work. When the bill is paid and the games ready to be picked up, they are assembled, boxed, shrink-wrapped, packed in shipping boxes and all set to sell.

Or, at your option, you may choose to collect the printed items yourself and take them around to the various vendors who will make them into boxes, boards, card decks, rule books, and whatever else you need. Then you are going to have to retrieve these pieces as they are finished and take them to wherever the games are to be assembled, where each piece will be left gathering dust until the last item arrives. Then they will be assembled and shrink-wrapped.

If the game is handled this latter way, using different vendors for different functions, you increase the chance of errors and substitute your time and labor for the printer's. If at all possible it's best to provide the printer with all the artwork, then let him handle the rest. That includes everything from doing the four-color process separations to providing the finished products ready to ship. This is the better way to work for a couple of reasons. It becomes the printer's responsibility to make certain everything is the right size and arrives on time. And it frees you for the more important task of marketing. You will develop enough headaches from trying to sell the game. You don't need to lose sleep worrying whether the box wrap fits the box, the board fits in the box, and the box fits in the carton.

Who Is Responsible for What?

While we are on the subject of responsibility, be aware the printer is not responsible for proofreading and catching typographical errors. He will provide several proofs before the job actually goes to press. There will be bluelines, match prints, and all types of camera-produced sheets to examine. They are not being done to squeeze extra dollars from your budget. The printer does them for self-preservation. It is your responsibility to catch the errors. The printer will not print anything until you have approved the proofs and signed them to show that you have examined them thoroughly. So, proofread everything and measure everything. Don't assume that *anything* is right until you have done this. Once approved and printed it's too late. You have bought it!

When the subject of money comes up, make your position clear. Explain that you have opened an escrow account at a bank and that an irrevocable letter of credit will be issued guaranteeing payment upon delivery. If the printer is not satisfied with this arrangement, go elsewhere. Remember that it is going to take about 45 days to complete the game (not including time for custom plastics) and there is no point in losing interest on your money during this time.

The Power of a Letter of Credit

The bank will probably charge a fee to issue the letter of credit (LC) but the LC's strength may justify the cost. The LC guarantees the printer he will be paid if you accept the games—no if's, ands, or buts. You may want to explain to the printer that providing him this security is costing you money in the form of bank fees. While you don't mind doing it, since the printer is guaranteed to be paid anyway, you would like to make the letter of credit payable 30 days after you accept delivery.

The printer is still guaranteed the money, the payment time is still reasonable, and it gives you 30 days to sell product and begin reclaiming your investment before parting with your money.

If you do not arrange an LC you probably will be required to pay 50% of the total cost as a deposit and pay the balance when the games are completed.

Unless you discover a printer you can trust right off the bat, try to get no fewer than three estimates. If one of the printers has a reputation for producing games and the others involved in the bidding do not, chances are the experienced printer's bid will be slightly higher than the other two. If the difference is not over 10%, consider giving him the job because of his expertise.

Beware of *Too* Low Estimates

Unfortunately, as in every profession, there are some printers who are less than honest. They will give an unsuspecting individual, one who is not familiar with the game industry, an exceptionally low bid to get the job, and later try to inflate the price once the work is half completed. If you get several quotes and one of them is substantially lower than the others, it would be prudent to be a little suspicious. A little additional checking on the printer's history might be wise.

A final word for those brave souls who intend to try and save a little extra cash by handling each phase of their game's production. If you are not content to let the printer do the entire job for you, it's entirely possible that you will be able to get by with what you have learned in this book. However, you will be a lot better off if you also have read at least one book on printing and another on box making. You also should plan on spending a lot more time on the project than you might expect and doing it during normal business hours, for this is when the trade shops are open.

Time doing what? First, you will have to run around to several box makers, scheduling appointments with each of them as you did with the printers. It's best to select the printer first so that he can coordinate dimensions. After you decide on a box maker, find someone to fabricate the gameboard. These people take a thick piece of cardboard, glue a piece of black paper to one side of it, neatly wrap the edges of the paper around the edge of the board, and then glue a printed game board sheet to the other side. This will be one of the most expensive items in the game.

When trying to find a company to do this, make sure they have a laminating machine capable of doing the work. If they are planning on doing it by hand and are producing more than 2,000 games, you probably will find that you won't be satisfied with either the cost, the time involved, or the degree of accuracy.

Once your suppliers are lined up and coordinated, find someone to make the corrugated shipping cartons. Next, find someone to assemble and shrink-wrap the game. If doing 2,500 games or less, consider buying inexpensive shrink-wrap equipment and doing the job yourself —if you have enough space to receive and store all the components until they can be assembled. Remember, an empty game box takes up the same amount of room as a full one. Until all the components are assembled and boxed, you will need approximately twice as much storage room as you will for the finished games.

Pay Attention to Shrink-Wrapping

Do not skip shrink-wrapping. You may think products are shrink-wrapped only to convince customers they are getting new, unused merchandise, but that is not entirely true. There are less expensive ways to seal packages. Shrink wrapping is important because the plastic film protects the package from scuffing in transit. Consumers don't want to buy a package that looks as though it has been through the postal system four or five times. Shrink wrap keeps that game box label looking beautiful and new.

If you are doing the game on your own, handling the components with various manufacturers, box makers, printers, and the like, always remember the cardinal rule: *You* are ultimately responsible. If something goes wrong you may become the subject of a story like this.

Your gameboards are delivered. Instead of the 10,000 you ordered there are only 8,300, but the bill is almost as high as if 10,000 had been finished. You call the board maker. Yes, he says, you are short, but it is not his fault. The board label paper was curled when he received it. The curl in the paper caused his normal spoilage rate of 7% to jump to nearly 20%. Not only are you short boards, but he is charging you for the excess raw chipboard lost because of increased spoilage. You call the printer. No, he says, the gameboard labels were fine when they left him. Sorry, it's not his fault either.

You can spend the rest of your life assigning blame but the net result is you are out 17% of your game boards and the money to make them. You can't assemble 17% of the other components you have paid for and you have lost 17% of gross sales potential.

Legally you will have an extremely difficult time forcing either the printer or the board maker to make good for the ruined boards. Because you essentially acted as a broker, *you* are ultimately responsible for the project.

On the other hand, if you contract with one manufacturer to produce the entire game you are transferring ultimate responsibility to that single source vendor. If they are 17% short, at the very least you will not have to pay for any of the 17% components that cannot be assembled and sold (not just the bad boards). And if the vendor realizes he's going to lose 17% of his billing it is more than likely he will make up the difference at his expense.

This is one of the most compelling reasons to contract your game's production with a single vendor source—at least with your first game. But if you do, make absolutely certain the single vendor you select has a sterling reputation as a private label game contract manufacturer.

If you do it yourself ... If you can face it all cheerfully, singing favorite old songs as you assemble mountains (that never seem to diminish in size) of game elements, doing it on your own will probably save you some money on very short print runs and in the short run. It is going to cost more in the long term, however, because you could have been—and should have been—spending all that time on marketing, the activity that matters the most.

A WORD ABOUT CARD GAMES

If the game you are thinking of doing is a card game (one comprised of cards, a sheet of rules, and a package) the road becomes at once simple, but also difficult.

It's simple because of the few components involved and the relatively easy time you will have locating vendors of these components. Your production costs generally should be far lower than if you had produced a typical board game. When your requirements are simple playing cards that must be shuffled and dealt frequently, it isn't difficult at all to find the names of various manufacturers in directories or other business references.

The Competition Is Tough

Your difficulties will arise when you attempt to market your game in competition with the publishers who manufacture hundreds of thousands of decks of cards at a time. Their economies of scale enable them to retail a single deck at a price equal to your production costs. To add to your frustration, you should realize that some of the people who produce the kinds of playing cards you need are the same competitors you will have to face in the retail market. They are some of the very few firms with the equipment necessary for economically printing, round corner cutting, collating, and plastic wrapping a deck of cards. They are the very firms, in short, engaged in producing and selling card games in the market place. They will produce for other companies as well, but somehow the price, regardless of quantity, never seems to be competitive with their own products.

It is also a little inconvenient that many of these firms are limited as to the size and number of cards they can produce per deck. When dealing with them make sure to ask for specifications early on in your discussions. If your requirements are 90 cards per deck but the equipment only makes 56-card decks, something has to change.

Quality Needs and Considerations

When you are looking for card deck manufacturers, you may come across a number of card manufacturers who make things like direct market post card packs, baseball collector cards, and trivia-style game cards. They certainly have the equipment to make a stack of cards, but be sure they have the other equipment necessary to not only round-corner the cards but to make a playing card deck quality edge where the sides of the deck feel relatively smooth to the touch.

On the other hand, if your card game uses "draw" cards—those which are left in a deck to be drawn and played one at a time—they probably will not need to be round-cornered, plastic-coated, and wrapped into individual decks. In this case, it should be easy to locate firms with machines called card slitters and collators. They provide a broad range of sizes and numbers of cards in individual decks.

Since we have pretty much established that a card game from a new company cannot compete head-on with the card game giants, it becomes necessary to compete on levels other than price. Packaging becomes more important than ever. The independently-produced game has to sell for more and it has to look like it is worth more. In other words, you have to sell the sizzle, not just the steak.

Important: Changing Card Game Market Demographics

The game industry's changing nature may present specific opportunities in the years ahead, and young companies may be positioned to exploit those opportunities.

While there is a definite trend toward electronic literacy, including in the game field, demographics demonstrate seniors will be the country's single largest age group at the turn of the century. People in this age range not only grew up playing and continue to play board games, they spend many pleasurable hours playing such card games as *Canasta*, Rummy, Gin, Bridge, Whist, Hearts, Spades, and Pinochle. While they still play those old favorites today, relative newcomers like *UNO*, *Skip-Bo*, and *Set* sell a million copies or more every year.

International Games—the producers of *UNO* (4 million units per year and more than 100 million since 1970), *Skip-Bo* (1.5 million per year), *Rage*, *Baha*, and *Trumpet*—dominates the adult card game market. In the late 70s they cultivated this market aggressively. Eventually they took business from other major manufacturers, none of whom fought very hard to stay in that market.

Why didn't those companies fight to stay in the adult card game market? Because their businesses changed. Through mergers, buy-outs, and competitor pressure they became driven by quarterly profits. The only way for them to generate substantial short-term profit increases is to promote heavily. New games from these companies often have two to three dollars per unit built into the wholesale price to cover advertising costs. This works fine for an item wholesaling to Toys-R-Us, K-Mart, and Wal-Mart for $14.95, but it costs the same to advertise a $6.00 card game on TV as it does a $20.00 board game. Clearly they cannot hide two or three dollars of advertising cost in a card game.

International Games, then privately held, won by default. They were willing to spend the time developing non-promoted card games. Today, like the other publicly held industry giants, they are driven by the need for quarterly profits. Don't misunderstand. International

Games is far from abandoning adult card games, but they are diversifying. That diversity, and other companies' lack of attention to this market may present you with an opportunity.

In tough economic times, or without huge media budgets to guide them, consumers only buy high-end products which they know and trust. *MONOPOLY*, *Clue*, *Risk*, *SCRABBLE*, *CANDY LAND*, *Life*, and other traditional games continue to sell strongly in a market where virtually everything else is down. Consumers seem more likely to try a new product in the low to medium price range.

To that point, there appears to be an opening in the market for a properly positioned, low end line of non-promoted adult games. How do you take advantage of this. It isn't easy and nothing is certain, but here is how I would approach it.

Let's assume you have a good card game. Jazz it up a little. Add a mini-gameboard or some clever pieces used in the game's play. Design a package that would be large enough to hold four card decks two by two. When the consumer gets your product home they will find two or three neatly wrapped decks of cards and whatever extra component you have incorporated into the gameplay. You have created perceived value. The consumer will pay more for it because it is worth more. That is how you sell your card game for $12.00 when the big companies are selling theirs for five or six dollars.

Card games take a long time to develop in the market place. Because of the low end retail and accordingly low wholesale cost, you cannot afford to spend much on advertising. So how do some companies make it? Here's how two products became successful.

A woman named Hazel Bowman from a Texas border town invented a card game based on *Double Solitaire*. She called the game *Skip-Bo* and offered it to International Games. They politely refused it, explaining how hard it is to establish card games. Undaunted, Ms. Bowman manufactured a few thousand copies and hit the road. She and her retired husband drove their motor home to every KOA campground and retirement center between Phoenix and Key West. They crisscrossed the sun belt a dozen times in three years, playing and selling their game in every town they could find on a map.

It was slow going. The first year they lost a *lot* of money. The second year they had some sales but the financial hole was getting deeper. In the third year they began to see a little light. In year four they broke even. In the fifth year, International Games called and wanted to talk. Ms. Bowman licensed the product and now collects royalties on over a million units a year. Not a bad retirement income!

A few years later another retiree named Edna Graham met Hazel Bowman, heard her story and said to herself, "I can do that." She reasoned *Skip-Bo* was really only a twist on *Double Solitaire*, a game already popular among seniors. Edna looked around for another favorite, settled on Dominoes, not a card game but one played by as many senior citizens. She added a twist and a few special pieces, called it *Spinner*, and hit the road.

After three years of non-stop motor home promotion, the game began to take off. Edna passed away in 1992 but her game lives on. The company that has it now is amazed at how fast its sales are growing.

As I said, it isn't easy ... but it can be done. These two stories prove it.

Your game may be far better than anything the big companies have on retailers' shelves and it may be worth more money, but consumers seeing the item for the first time won't know this. All they will notice is that one card game sells for $4.99 and the other one for $12.95. There has to be some discernible difference between the two, either in packaging or in the promise of the game itself, to provide $12.95 worth of fun the first time it is played. That is why it is essential not only to make the package larger but to incorporate legitimately some small component other than cards into the gameplay to separate the product from your less expensive competitors.

Exploiting Non-Traditional Target Markets

I have a client who produced a card game called *Construction Chase*, which deals with the housing industry. It consists of two decks of 56 cards each, a set of rules, and a cleverly designed box. However, you will not find it easily in normal card game outlets. After listening to some sage advice, the inventors decided not to attack the traditional markets but to concentrate on a specialty target—the construction/real estate market.

Because of the number of firms and people engaged in the industry, this is one of the country's largest specialty markets. The game sells for $10 and at last check was doing extremely well, being sold to firms as a gift item and to retail and wholesale outlets that never carried games before. By the time the specialty market is exhausted the game will have had time to establish itself and then it may be possible to make a relatively easy transition into the traditional markets.

The point is card games can and do work, and sometimes they work better in less competitive, non-traditional markets where they can command a higher price.

MAKING COMPUTER GAMES

I have done some things in my life I don't really regret doing but would never do again—not for any amount of fame, fortune, or political power. One of these things is attempting a start-up of a computer software game company.

If an individual combines the talents of a genius computer programmer, a brilliant game designer, and an extremely clever business person, maybe—but only maybe—the computer game market could hold more than empty promises. But if any one of these talents is missing, that person is well advised to avoid this market completely.

Ten years ago (even five years ago), the computer software market was wide open. Existing companies could not obtain new programs fast enough to feed a voracious market. Everything was sold while it was new. Retail prices were spectacularly high, as were profit margins, and when rapidly evolving hardware technology made an older program obsolete, it was easy enough to drop the old game from the line and replace it with a new one. It was great fun; a financial/technological roller coaster ride with enough thrills and rewards to keep everyone happy.

But the ride ended. The market became glutted pretty quickly, littered with the debris of second rate software. The successful companies, those still around today, began to spend extravagantly on advertising for their newest products. Eventually, the market evolved into one dominated by promotional spending; he who spent the most sold the most. But sometimes that spending turned out to be disproportionate to the sales and revenues obtained . . . and another company bit the dust.

Like the board game market, the computer game market today is dominated by a few large firms who have managed to weather the storms; companies who consistently produce quality products supported by strong marketing budgets.

Still Want to Try It? If the computer game market looks like an entrepreneurial challenge you would like to accept, you may want to give it a shot. However, if you do not have the funds to promote your game heavily, don't waste your time.

Still want to give it a try? Your game/program had better be first rate and your computer graphics state of the art, and be warned that last year's "state of the art" may well be passé this year). Remember the perceived value of the game is shaped in the consumer's mind during the first few minutes of playing time.

Another consideration is the need for consumer support personnel. Ask any company making software what their biggest headache is, and most will answer without a second's hesitation. Consumer support. You need trained personnel to answer questions from people who call, thinking there is something wrong with the software. In fact, they are trying to run it on the wrong hardware or simply did not read the instructions.

Your software packaging and advertising graphics must compete effectively against high standards. Their quality must reflect this. Fortunately, there is still a substantial profit margin available once the product has been established, and the software can support a substantial packaging expense. Remember that other than the packaging, all the customer is getting is a flat disk.

Another concern is disk reproduction itself. The price of disks has come down substantially in the past few years, as has the cost of copying or duplicating. Experience demonstrates even the quality oriented firms have a relatively high rate of defective products. Fly-by-night companies who use the cheapest disks and copying services find themselves replacing disks faster than they can sell new ones. It pays to pay for and maintain quality.

One final word, before we move on to the critically important subject of marketing. The software business is full of barely adequate programmers; individuals who know just enough to pass themselves off as experts to those who are truly novices. Each of us possesses certain fundamental personality traits which help us to be successful in some areas and prevent us from achieving great success in others. It is my belief that the characteristics that make a person a great game inventor are almost diametrically opposed to those which make a person a brilliant programmer. A person who has both is as rare as hen's teeth.

Unless you can program at least a little and understand the language of this business, stay away from the software game business. The odds are stacked heavily against you.

PART 6: Marketing

If there is only one section of this book you take to heart it should be this one.

Making a game is a lot like having a baby. Conceiving it is fun, but it doesn't take very long. What follows is a long, drawn out gestation period during which the seed of an idea develops into an embryo and finally emerges as a baby — a new product. The proud parents show their new product to everyone they know. They tell of miserable nights and family hardships, all the things they went through to bring their baby into the world. Usually at this point new parents realize the real work has just begun. True, it took nine months to produce the baby but they are going to be raising it for the next eighteen years.

Regardless of how much effort you put into inventing and designing your game, and raising the money to manufacture it, and regardless of the impossible obstacles, negative reactions, and hardships you overcame to get the product to the market it all pales when compared to meeting the marketing challenge — and doing what ultimately will determine whether your game succeeds or . . .

Sad to say, I have seen a number of remarkably good games shrivel and die because the entrepreneur/inventor did not have the money or know-how to launch the product correctly. On the other hand, there have been a few really awful games that lasted far longer than they should have because some persuasive marketing whiz knew how to launch a product.

Before you can market any product you must have a fundamental understanding of the product's market dynamics. Games are no exception. The game market may share similarities with other product markets, but there are differences. Some of them are subtle, some are not. Not understanding the market or not heeding the differences is a short-cut to failure. It is not enough to plan on selling your game to the same people who bought *Trivial Pursuit* or *PICTIONARY*. You must examine the market, segment the population of consumers and retailers, and create a viable marketing plan that will show specifically who you will be selling your product to during the various phases of its life cycle. You must realistically identify retailers ranging from those least likely to buy a new game from an emerging company to those who are hungry for this type of product. In short, you had better get educated fast. Lack of marketing knowledge is the number one reason most self-publishers fail.

MARKET DYNAMICS

Self-publishers find themselves crushed between diametrically opposed market dynamics. To anyone who has really examined the industry, they are fairly straightforward and simple. Most newcomers simply ignore them or refuse to believe they will impact their product. They are wrong.

For twenty years I have attended the annual American International Toy Fair. It is the largest toy show in the United States and an extremely important show for launching a game on a national basis. The show is attended by almost 20,000 retailers, manufacturers, sales representatives, inventors, and packagers — and anyone else who conducts any kind of business with the toy industry. Toy Fair is held in three New York City locations: the Toy Building at 200 Fifth Avenue; the adjoining building at 1107 Broadway (both buildings are permanent show rooms), and the Jacob Javits Convention Center. (In addition some of the giant toy companies, like Hasbro and Mattel, have their own buildings nearby.)

The Bad News: Most New Game Companies Fail

Since I earn a living by knowing who is manufacturing what games I spend ten to twelve days each February rooting through these buildings, visiting exhibitors and trying to keep tabs on all the players. Because I keep in contact with these companies through letters it is important to keep an accurate mailing list. Which brings us to the point.

Every year at Toy Fair I uncover an average of one hundred new game companies; not new games, new game companies. All of these are dutifully added to the mailing list. One year later, at the next Toy Fair, eighty of last year's crop of new companies are gone. Two years later only two are still exhibiting at Toy Fair. And this is not saying they have been successful, only that they have survived.

This is the first dynamic force at work on a new game company. You are entering an industry that, statistically speaking, destroys 98% of all new game companies within 24 months of their inception. Very few other businesses are that brutal. The second dynamic force operating on new game companies involves, strangely enough, some good news.

The Better News: Most Blockbuster Games Are Developed by Entrepreneurs

Trivial Pursuit, PICTIONARY, DUNGEONS & DRAGONS, Pente, UNO, Skip-Bo, MONOPOLY, and just about every other blockbuster game you can name came from the inventor/entrepreneurial sector. Not one of them originated within a major game company. All of them were self-published and placed into a hostile, over-crowded market place where, for some reason, they not only survived but eventually thrived.

If you look at how long these games were aggressively marketed before they became successful, you will discover they were being sold and promoted for an average of four years. There are a few exceptions.

PICTIONARY made it big in three years and *Trivial Pursuit* in three and a half years. However, *UNO* and *DUNGEONS & DRAGONS* took seven years, *MONOPOLY* six. The average is four years.

It doesn't take a genius to understand the implications of the opposing forces. On one hand we have an industry that kills ninety-eight percent of all new companies within twenty-four months. On the other hand, the same industry seems to require a product to survive for an average of four years before it can become a hit. See what I mean by diametrically opposed?

While surviving in this milieu may appear to be impossible, clearly it is not. After all we just named half a dozen games which made their inventors multi-millionaires.

I am not about to reveal some mystical guiding principle that will guarantee success. If I could, I probably would not be writing this book. I would be on one of my yachts trying to figure out how to live long enough to spend all my money. In fact, beware of any charlatan who claims to have a simple answer to marketing a game successfully. There isn't one.

What I am going to do is explain the market by breaking it down into its various elements and show how a product works in each.

PRODUCT LIFE CYCLES

All products have life cycles. Big companies like Procter & Gamble, IBM, and Quaker Oats, as well as big toy companies, have charts showing product life cycles for everything from shampoo to new breakfast cereals to twenty million dollar mainframe computers. Products' life cycles are similar in that there is an inclining curved line showing the amount of time it takes for the product to reach maturity then a declining line showing when the product levels off and eventually dies.

A Movie, for Example

When a new movie is released successfully, for example, its life cycle incline is nearly straight up. The majority of the advertising money is spent just before and during the film's release. People flock to theaters for a couple of weeks, then the life cycle decline line plummets as the movie is pulled from theaters. Later there is another sharp rise when the film is released for video rental and sales. That blip tapers off quickly and another appears when the movie shows up on cable.

The last blip in the cycle is when the film reaches commercial television. After that, barring a sequel or some cult following, the movie's life cycle plays itself out with a low but constant amount of rentals and revenues from late night TV movies.

A Game Life Cycle is Different

A game's life cycle curve is quite different. While the major companies may spend several million dollars promoting a new game, its sales usually do not leap off the chart. If the product is successful in the first year, word of mouth advertising combines with next year's ad budget to strengthen sales. If it has a good second year, it has a chance at a long life. On the other hand if a game *is* successful one year, its sales rarely plummet the next. Usually they decline steadily until they reach a demand plateau.

During *Trivial Pursuit*'s biggest year, it grossed something like $440,000,000. It has suffered an enormous decline but today, because of steady demand and good market husbandry, it still grosses $15,000,000 a year. I don't know if that would meet your expectations, but I could live very happily with $15,000,000 in annual sales. If it is handled properly, a successful game becomes an annuity that requires very little promotion to maintain itself in the market.

What has been discussed are the life cycles of successful products. If a product is simply a bad idea, or suffers because of cruel circumstances or terrible timing, it will crash and burn. There will be no inclining curve to product maturity. If you release your game and cannot make any headway, you may have to consider it was a bad idea, cut your losses, and make the most dignified exit possible.

MARKET TIERS DEFINED

The traditional game market can be divided into three tiers. It is important to understand the composition and workings of each tier or groups of sales outlets to increase your chances for success.

The first tier has the broadest base. It consists of independent toy, hobby, and game stores; small toy and game store chains; book, department, gift and novelty, drug and grocery, general merchandise, auto, and home supply stores; and catalog and mail order businesses. All of these retailers combined account for about eighteen percent (18%) of all games sold in the United States.

The second tier is made up of a narrow band of larger retail chains. Kay Bee Toys, K&K Toys, Hills, Bradlees, Circus World, Play World, Child World, and Leisure City are some of the twenty accounts that comprise this tier, which produces thirty percent (30%) of U.S. game sales.

The third tier is composed of discounters like K-Mart, Wal-Mart, Target, and Zayre's. This group controls thirty-three percent (33%) of game sales in the United States.

Let's add this all up: Tier one (18%) + Tier two (30%) + Tier three (33%) = 81%. What's missing? Look back through the list of companies in each tier and the missing name leaps to mind—Toys-R-Us. Toys-R-Us represents approximately 19% of all games sold in this country.

Three Tiers Plus One —Toys-R-Us

Toys-R-Us is treated as a separate market category because they are different. They are a toy chain, so they could be placed in tier two. They are a discounter, so they could also fit into the third tier. They sometimes try new unproven items, which gives them a characteristic in common with tier one. However, the main reason they should be treated separately is because they are such a dominant force in the industry and because they operate under their own rules.

Market Tiers Examined

Defining the three tiers and creating a special niche for Toy-R-Us can be done in a fairly straightforward manner. Understanding how each works and fits within the game market is a little more complicated. Let's look at each group.

Tier One: Independent and Small Chain Retailers

Independent toy and game stores carry a broad product selection which makes them a prime target for games from new companies. They hate to compete with discounters who carry heavily promoted games from major publishers and they usually are willing to give a quality game a chance. These stores prefer to order six or less of any given game, depending on how fast it is moving.

Small toy and game retail chains are another group to move in on right away. They also carry a wide product selection and are always looking for interesting new items. Some chains tend to specialize. The Gamekeeper obviously specializes in games and is always on the lookout for anything in the category. On the other hand, the Imaginarium focuses more on preschool and educational games. As you travel to conventions and make sales calls, study stores at every opportunity. When you later make your sales presentation, showing how your product truly fits the store's theme will give you a better chance of making the sale.

Bookstores can go either way. Some bookstore chains, like Waldenbooks and B. Dalton, have very small game departments which expand and contract seasonally. They tend to offer genre games, such as fantasy and science fiction role playing, which are cross supported by novels, or games which are connected to reading or words in some way. Some bookstores simply do not carry games.

DEPARTMENT STORES

Department stores can be good places in which to launch a new game. They tend to look for new, quality items which are not yet selling through discounters. They also try to be on retail's cutting edge, looking for the unique, the avant garde. The trouble is the cutting edge has two sides. When your product is new and different, they will consider buying and promoting it. Once the newness wears off, however — even if they have done well with it the year before—they may drop it simply because it is old.

A positive factor in selling to department store chains is that they place larger orders than independent retailers do. Neiman Marcus is an example with which I am familiar. If they bring your game in for the Christmas season and place it chain wide (24 stores), you could expect them to sell 3-400 units without promotion. If you help them promote the store in their five flagship stores you could expect sales of up to six hundred units. If you promote and they select it for the Neiman's Christmas catalog (they usually only put one or two games in the catalog), you might sell between twelve hundred and two thousand copies. Multiply these sales figures by ten department store chains and the numbers become quite interesting.

GIFT AND NOVELTY STORES

Gift and novelty stores are very iffy. Many have games on their shelves but they tend to carry chess, checkers, backgammon, and other commodity type games which range in price from very cheap $1.95 imports from China to high quality, hand finished wooden or stone sets that sell for hundreds of dollars. Spencer Gifts is a major gift & novelty chain that carries board games, but even they tend to specialize in products of an adult nature that retail for under $20.00.

The sheer numbers of gift stores make this a dangerous market. To successfully sell this group (and to avoid wasting a lot of time and effort), you must develop a strategy that eliminates those that are not likely to buy your product.

GROCERY AND DRUG STORES

There are more than 160,000 grocery and drug stores in the United States. Most of them retail some games. Unfortunately, they are not apt to be your sort. They tend to be interested only in "classics" (also called staples); games like *MONOPOLY, SCRABBLE, Parcheesi*, etc. They seldom carry any other type game unless it is heavily promoted. Remember that their principal business is selling food or drug items; games contribute only a tiny fraction of their business.

GENERAL MERCHANDISE STORES

General merchandise stores (Woolworth's, M.E. Moses, Etc.) offer a selection of games very much like that offered by grocery stores. It is such a small part of their business they are not interested in pioneering product. Consequently they do not represent fertile ground for new game companies.

AUTO AND HOME SUPPLY STORES

Auto and home supply stores (Home Depot, Western Auto, etc.) sometimes sell games. Usually they tend to be more interested in the outdoor variety; for example, horseshoes, badminton, and ring toss. It is rare for them to stock any board games.

MAIL ORDER/CATALOG BUSINESSES

As of this writing, there are 7,227 mail order/catalog businesses in the United States. More than 3,000 of them sell toys and games. Catalog and mail order represent excellent opportunities for some new games. Like department stores they often seek high quality, trend setting merchandise that does not compete with what K-Mart is promoting at a discount.

Tier Two—National Toy Chain Retailers

This group of retailers is made up of national chains that focus on toys and games. Kay Bee, K&K, and Circus World are examples of these stores. Their outlets usually are located in malls or other high retail traffic areas. A visit to any one of them quickly reveals they are not pioneers. New products from new companies are rare. 80% of their shelf space is stocked with merchandise from maybe a dozen companies. The products they carry are staples (long established items like *MONOPOLY, Clue*, and *SCRABBLE*), some current releases from major companies, and a handful of heavily promoted items. While it is possible for a new company to break into this group it probably is not advisable to do it before the company is able to sustain product demand on a national level.

Tier Three—National Discount Chain Retailers

This is the short list. K-Mart, Wal-Mart, Target, and one or two other discount chains control a huge percentage of the game business. Even the major companies hotly compete for space in their limited game departments. To understand why being successful in selling to them is so tough, you have to understand the concept of discount stores.

First, they are called discounters for good reason. The underpinning principle of their business is to sell name brand merchandise at less than full retail. That is their reputation and that is the reason customers walk through their doors.

In order to make this work, they carry products which exist in a *pre-sold* condition. Pre-sold means customers are walking in stores all across the nation and looking or asking for a specific product. If it is an established product like *MONOPOLY* or *SCRABBLE*, it may not be promoted at all other than by years of built up consumer demand. If it is a "hot" product, the demand is created either by word-of-mouth or by paid promotion. In any case, people are walking into discount stores across the country looking for a particular game. When this condition exists, these stores are willing to carry your game.

ADVANTAGES AND DISADVANTAGE OF PRE-SOLD GAMES

But be very careful. If a product is pre-sold as a result of an advertising or publicity campaign, the consumer demand usually evaporates within 48 hours of the campaign's end. All those ready to spend consumers lining up to buy a product disappear. Selling to these stores before you can sustain demand is dangerous. If your product is not successful enough to be brought back in for the next Christmas season, you may find yourself out in the cold.

A few years ago two ladies teamed up to manufacture and market a clever word game. It was an old game with a new twist; a lot of fun, well packaged, and at a good price point. The ladies did not have a huge budget, but they were fire balls. For two and half years they substituted creativity, energy, and contagious enthusiasm for the money they did not have.

The game was not a giant success but it was doing nicely in about 400 Tier One retail accounts when disaster struck. Both women were mothers with children who became teenagers during the time they were devoting 110% of their energies to their game. Deciding they had to spend more time with their families, they needed to bring in outside help to establish their game more quickly in Tier's Two and Three.

BEWARE OF SLICK MARKETERS

They found their help in the form of a slick marketer. Armed with expensive Mont Blanc pens, clad in Armani suits, and mounting a leased Mercedes he charged in and took control. He quickly informed me that no longer would it be business as usual. He implied that the marketing advice I had given the ladies, while prudent, was old fashioned and out of style. "The market place has changed," he informed me. "If you want to be successful you have to start at the top. Don't worry about the mom & pop stores. They are dinosaurs who just don't know they are extinct," he said.

I listened patiently, trying to keep from reaching across the table and strangling this pompous jerk. I had worked with the lady inventors for two and a half years. I liked them and wanted them to be successful, in spite of this stuffed Italian silk suit telling me I didn't have the foggiest idea what I was doing and that within one year he would have the game in K-Mart.

When he finished I cautiously tried to make the point, that unless he was bringing a steamer trunk full of hundred dollar bills to the party (I knew he was not), the game had not developed enough to be successful in discount stores. I further gently reminded him that an abortive entry into discounters would almost certainly have a negative impact on all those "worthless" mom & pop accounts upon whose success the business was built.

He looked at me as if I had just proven his point; i.e., I had no idea how this business worked. Unable to resist, I added, "It's true that I have only been involved with just over 150 games in the last 18 years, and the one thing I know about this industry is that I learn something new every day. Just out of curiosity, how many games have you marketed before?"

"Well, only one game," he replied, "but plenty of other consumer items. Anyway, it's not the quantity that matters, it's the quality."

"I couldn't agree more," I responded. "So what was the one game? Is it in K-Mart or Toys-R-Us? Where could I buy a copy?"

As you may have guessed, the one game (if there ever was one) was not only no longer on the market, I had never heard of it.

I will give credit where credit is due. Even though I thought he was dead wrong, full of himself, and bringing about the demise of the product the inventors worked hard to establish, he did get the game into K-Mart nine months later. I don't know how many lies and promises he made to get the order but the bottom line is he was good enough to convince K-Mart not only to put it on their shelves but to promote it in two of their Christmas advertisements.

THE GOOD NEWS . . .

We shipped nearly 60,000 games to K-Mart in October and November. Everyone was looking at me like I was an idiot and even I was beginning to give that theory some credibility. Christmas came and went. When January 10, the invoice payment date, rolled by without a check from K-Mart, the marketer called to hustle up payment and get another order. He was disappointed. The check was on its way but was being held pending the K-Mart buyer asking the marketer for "mark-down" money (funds used to offset K-Mart's lowering the price in an effort to unload excess inventory). K-Mart had sold 40,000 copies of the game but were left with the balance—20,000. If they could not send them back they needed mark-down money

The marketer got his money but never another K-Mart order. There was still a warehouse full of back-up inventory for those K-Mart re-orders that never came. Relative to the amount of promotion it received, the game had not performed to the expected level of sales. Having come close to victory and tasted the champagne, the marketer did not want to give up. He decided moving to get into K-Mart prematurely had been a tactical mistake. He would continue to gain grass roots support through Tier One outlets, then attack the discounters in another year.

AND THE BAD NEWS . . .

Wrong! Great concept, but he had shot himself in the foot. The Tier One retailers, faced with K-Mart's price and promotion competition and left completely unsupported for the entire Christmas season, turned their collective backs on the product. As far as they were concerned, K-Mart had satisfied completely the product's limited demand. There was no reason for them to pioneer an item which had already been a K-Mart "Blue Light Special".

Sadly, the game died. There was nothing that could have been done short of wasting millions of dollars on television ads to lure other discounters to issue purchase orders. It just about broke the inventors' hearts, but it was over. Two and a half years of carefully nurturing the product in the market had been wasted because someone was successful at getting the product into a discounter *too early in the game's life cycle.*

Toys-R-Us

Toys-R-Us has their own section here not only because they are big (controlling 19% of the game market) but because they are different.

They are one of the most highly computerized retail chains in the world. When the clerk scans the UPC bar code on an item that information is not only transmitted instantly to the cash register but it also goes to corporate headquarters where it becomes one of the millions of pieces of information that make up the Toys-R-Us inventory control program. What does the Toys-R-Us system mean to you?

Unlike discounters who have a very limited selection of games, Toys-R-Us stores offer hundreds of titles. A virtual wall of games down the length of the store gives them opportunities to try products other chains would not. If you check carefully, you will find most of their games, probably 80%, come from Milton Bradley, Parker Brothers, Mattel, Pressman Toy, Western Publishing, and TYCO Toys. But you will also discover whole product lines from such companies as University Games, Tiger Electronics, Cadaco, Cardinal Industries, and others. And occasionally you will find a game invented and manufactured by someone like yourself.

Manufacturers' representatives have a saying, "You can sell almost anything to Toys-R-Us ... once." Be very careful not to sell Toys-R-Us too soon. While they may be more open to new games than other discounters because of their broad selection, they are ultra sensitive to sell-through (movement of product from the store). They know exactly how many copies of an item they should sell in order to meet their minimum turn requirements. They may give your game a chance but if it doesn't sell at the projected rate, it will be out before you know it and you will find them extremely reluctant to even talk to you about bringing it back in later.

If you believe that if your game just gets on Toys-R-Us shelves across the country it will sell itself, you are dead wrong. 150 years ago you might have been right, but that was before someone invented marketing.

MARKETING: WHAT IS IT?

Back in the good old days, when our great grandfathers had little time for relaxation, people bought products with which they were familiar and happy or those recommended by trusted friends and relatives. If four brands of salt appeared on a merchant's shelf you can bet that only the best one, or possibly two, would be there in two months. People were suspicious of new things. Not like today when the word "new" is perceived as a product benefit.

One company that was around in those days was run by two partners; brothers-in-law, in fact, Mr. Procter and Mr. Gamble. They made candles and had just come off an economic high—providing candles to the Union army. With the end of the war came the end of the big government contracts. They were looking around for some other product they could add to their line which used many of the same raw materials and manufacturing facilities.

Marketing and Selling Soap

They felt as though they could make bath soap, but the soap companies already in business were old line, well established firms with many loyal consumers. Both men used soap themselves and knew how reluctant their wives were to try a new brand. They were pondering their predicament when one of the brothers found an article about a new technique called marketing. The idea was that through combining product, advertising, promotion, and sales, a company could convince consumers their product was better than the product they were currently using and get them to try it. If the product was better it was a guaranteed success. Even if it were only as good as what it replaced, it probably would still be the product of choice. Why? Because the customer already had been convinced through marketing it *was* the best choice.

The partners thought about it, cast caution to the winds, and started making and marketing soap. The rest is history.

The definition of marketing Messrs. Procter and Gamble read over a hundred years ago is still pretty applicable. The big marketing companies will tell you there is a whole lot more to it than that, and there is, but I think it pretty much captures the essence of what marketing is all about. Besides, Procter and Gamble seem to have done all right using it as a premise.

Webster defines marketing as "an aggregate of functions involved in moving goods from producer to consumer." That's pretty clear, but it doesn't help us much. To make sense of the definition, we need to break down that aggregate of functions and examine each one.

Think of your product as a rocket you are trying to launch. Marketing is the rocket's engine. The engine has three independent motors: Sales, Advertising and Promotions, each with its own thrust-producing nozzle. All systems are go. You count down and hit the launch button. If all three motors work together, the rocket lifts off, gradually gaining speed until it reaches escape velocity and goes into orbit. But if any one of the motors malfunction at lift-off or while climbing, the rocket is thrown off course. It will begin to wobble and then plummet back to earth, the victim of gravity.

Marketing's three elements—sales, advertising, and promotion—must work in synchronized harmony to launch your game successfully. If all goes well, the game's sales slowly begin to climb, then gradually increase until you have it firmly established in the marketplace.

Marketing vs. Selling

I have seen too many game inventors fall prey to slick, predatory marketing companies. There are companies in the game industry that set up attractive booths at trade shows, produce pretty four color catalog sheets, and lure game inventors with the words they want to hear: "Yes, we can do it all for you. When you choose us, we make your game, market it ... we do everything. All you have to do is sign on the dotted line and give me a check for $00000.00" (typically tens of thousands of dollars).

It is what inventors want to hear and unfortunately many fall victim to this form of abuse every year. The reason these companies can get away with this is that they do exactly what they say they are going to do—market the game. They don't sell it and they don't promote it; they market it. The next time you run into one of these slippery firms, pick up a copy of their catalog and take it with you to Toys-R-Us or any specialty store which stocks games. If you don't find a good percentage (at least 33%) of their products on these shelves then you know what you have found—a hollow marketing company.

What a real marketing company or division does is study the market, decide on a strategy that works within the budget, then establish and oversee sales, advertising, and promotions. Marketing is responsible for coordinating these three functions whether at trade shows, in-store demonstrations, or public relations events. Marketing's job is to make sure all the elements function in harmony. There are no guarantees of easy solutions or quick boosts to sagging sales.

But what of the other areas? Let's look at each.

Sales There used to be a sign over my desk that read, "Nothing happens until somebody sells something." The biggest manufacturing plant in the world would sit idle, gathering dust without a steady influx of orders. Orders are generated by selling product.

The sales arm of your game company has but one responsibility—to place product on store shelves. It should employ every available incentive to accomplish this mission. These incentives may be pricing discounts, in-store promotions, co-op advertising, public relations tours, media advertising; in short, all the sales stimuli created by marketing's other activities. Often manufacturers get upset with their sales people because they are not getting reorders. That's not their job. Their job is to get the product on the shelf. If reorders are not forthcoming, it probably is because the other marketing departments are not doing their job; i.e., getting consumers to buy the product from the stores.

If your sales force is having trouble getting initial placement and/or your accounts are not reordering, take a look at the effectiveness of your other two marketing functions before dumping the blame on your sales staff.

Speaking of sales staff, you were planning to hire a national sales manager and about six factory sales people weren't you? Of course not. Even if you could afford a staff like that it simply doesn't make economic sense when you only have one or two products to sell. What is more likely is that you will want to work with independent manufacturers' representatives (reps).

Obviously companies that buy large quantities of games are constantly besieged by everybody with anything to sell. They simply don't have the time to deal with all these new items. Consequently, a system has developed using reps. A rep is an independent agent who represents your game or line, as well as products from several other companies, for a sales commission. The rep's job is to act as sales liaison between manufacturers and higher volume buyers. However, just because reps have the ability to show your item to a buyer does not mean they will show it to the buyer every time they meet.

Reps have to be discriminating. They walk on a tightrope. If a rep knows a game is wrong for a buyer, he may be out a customer if he forces a buy. When the game does not sell for that particular buyer, the rep not only will lose future commissions on that game, he will lose them on the other dozen lines he offers. On the other hand, if the rep doesn't show and sell a manufacturer's item to enough buyers he is going to be fired and lose the line. Reps must constantly weigh the trust the buyer places in them vs. the obligation they have to the manufacturer.

In other cases it may be that the product is right for a particular buyer's stores but the buyer is not comfortable with the manufacturer's promotions and advertising or the factory's ability to deliver product. In this instance the rep is between a rock and a hard place. The factory wants the big order and pushes the rep to go back to the buyer. The buyer wants to know what is different from the last time he said no?

PROBLEMS WITH A ONE GAME LINE

Many reps simply are not interested in trying to sell a one-item line. They feel it is not worth their effort to try to carve out a niche in the marketplace for a single game. Here's why. Your rep has an appointment with a major buyer in his show room at the market center. The buyer has been working the toy fair for two days. He is tired and running behind. He is fifty minutes late when he comes in and tells the rep their two hour appointment is now one hour. The rep takes the buyer to his bicycle display and spends fifteen minutes getting a $200,000.00 order. He then goes to his outdoor pool toy line and, in 20 minutes, writes another $200,000.00 order. Next they visit the rep's action figures for another 20 minutes. The buyer sees a new item he likes and what the rep hoped would be a $100,000 order turns into $400,000.

The rep has five minutes left in his hour. He can either rush the buyer through one or two more major product lines and generate orders of $50,000 to $100,000 or he can spend the five minutes trying to explain your game and hope to get a $5,000 to $10,000 test order. Where would you take the buyer?

When a rep takes a line, he obtains exclusivity for a particular territory. If the rep's territory is the Midwest, then the rep gets paid his 10-15% commission on every item sold in any of his states—regardless of who actually made the sale. As in every other profession, there are good reps and there are bad reps. It has been demonstrated repeatedly that a bad rep is far worse than no rep at all. If you find yourself tied up with a bad rep (you'll know very quickly), fire him. Delaying will only make things worse.

Sales Manager

After more than twenty years and two hundred games I have not seen a single game succeed unless the person responsible for sales had a direct, vested interest in that success. If you turn your sales over to a national sales rep network or hire a legitimate marketing company you had better be prepared to conduct sales management responsibilities on a hands-on, day-to-day basis.

Selling the game may be the hardest, most grueling, most measurable task in the whole process. If the person doing it does not have a *to the bone* commitment, it is easy to become discouraged, make excuses, and slow down. The person responsible for this activity probably deserves the lion's share of credit if the game becomes successful. That person probably will be you or your partner.

OWNER—STAY INVOLVED IN SALES MANAGEMENT

Most people who have demonstrated they are good at selling games are already working and making more money than you can afford to pay them. If someone is looking for a job selling games it probably means he is currently unemployed because he was not successful for his last company. If you hire someone—anyone—to be a sales manager, he will be working for future money. Whether it is commission, salary, or a combination, he cannot really lose what he has not had. If things get tough he can slide along, making less money for a while, then move on. On the other hand, your company is at stake. If things get tough, not only will you make less money, you stand to lose everything you have put into the project. You have a little more motivation to make it work than anyone you can hire.

Don't get me wrong. You need all the help you can get and afford. From consultants to reps, to an employee to assist you in managing sales, anything that makes this job more productive is worth considering. But you must never imagine you can completely turn this role over to anyone else while the company is young.

If you are going to be the sales manager you need to be aggressive; not pushy, not abrasive, but relentlessly persistent. In fact I recently received a letter from a client who said that not only had I told the truth when I explained the importance of sales persistence but that the next time I told someone I should make it bold and underline it. **Be Persistent**.

Advertising

These can be dangerous waters. While cable, VCR's, the national literacy rate, population demographics, and a dozen other factors are co-alescing to change the effectiveness of media advertising, the consensus among major retailers and game manufacturers is that high priced television commercials are the only way to dramatically affect a game's sales development. Even this is changing as game companies maintain high television ad profiles by switching from very costly network ads to lower cost cable spots. The bottom line here is you probably cannot afford anything like a national television ad campaign ... and without national product distribution, you don't want one.

It also is a safe bet that even with a respectable budget, you cannot afford the waste inherent in working with large advertising agencies; that is, if you can find one that thinks your budget is big enough.

Once again, the responsibility comes home to roost. But it is a little easier than managing sales. This time, by doing a little research, a lot of planning, and being brilliantly creative you can come up with a master advertising plan that provides the versatility a small company needs at a budget that probably will be affordable.

The Nut Shell Advertising Plan

If you don't have national distribution, meaningful distribution, and it does not look as though you will for at least the first two years, any kind of national advertising would be ineffective.

What you need is a plan that will allow you to focus your funds in areas where the games are being sold. Pretend you pick Dallas. Depending on the game and the budget you can afford to place ads in the following: college newspapers, one or two small ads in the *Dallas Morning News*, maybe *D Magazine* or *Texas Monthly*, KRLD or KLIF talk radio stations, possibly even a package on a local UHF television channel.

Pretend your advertising budget is a bowling ball. If you get on a plane and fly to the middle of the Atlantic Ocean and drop it, not much happens—just a small splash lost in the waves. On the other hand if you take that same bowling ball and drop it into a rain puddle you can bet everyone at the bus stop will notice it. Focus your advertising plans and dollars. You can not afford to be wrong or ineffective.

Promotions

Most of the people I know are sick of being on the receiving end of advertising. I find it difficult to enjoy broadcast television because the ads are either insulting or offensive ... billboards are usually garish and boring ... you can almost smell the liquor and cigarette ads in those glossy magazines ... and doesn't it seem as though you wait forever between songs on your favorite radio station?

We are overdosed on product advertising. I have reached the point that when I am exposed to a particularly insulting or offending ad I write a note to the product's manufacturer. I tell them that while they may make an excellent product, this specific ad was stupid and/or offensive and they should let the people responsible know it.

What does this have to do with marketing your game? Lots.

Trivial Pursuit, PICTIONARY, UNO, Clever Endeavor, Spinner, and a slew of other successful games have been introduced to the market with a minimum of advertising but a maximum of promotion.

What's the difference? Advertising is somebody trying to buy your vote. Promotion is someone trying to earn your vote.

If people are presented with a newspaper advertisement for one game and a newspaper article for another competing game its likely they will choose the one featured in the article. We are all wary of advertising but we tend to trust news stories. Another example would be a choice between buying a game you saw pictured in a television commercial or one someone showed you how to play at a local retail outlet. In most cases the choice is easy. This means that when you can achieve them, effective promotions produce better results than equivalent advertising.

Sales, advertising, and promotion are all critical to a game's ultimate success. The greatest sales force in the world is wasted if the game is not advertised and promoted. All three must work together. The secret to making all three marketing arms function effectively in unison is planning.

PLANNING

It happens with frightening frequency. A potential client calls or comes in all aglow over his or her game and wants to have it manufactured. Part of my services include making packaging suggestions, and that requires I have an understanding of the game's basic market. I ask where and how do they plan to sell it?

Most of them look at me like I am a total idiot. "Why, to everyone," they answer; "the same people who buy *MONOPOLY*."

Having a kind nature and not wanting to earn a reputation as an unfeeling jerk, I gently explain my question by telling them I am aware they intend consumers to buy the product but are they going to try to start out selling it in every city in America ("Where are you going to sell the game?") and what type of marketing ("How are you going to sell it?") they will employ.

Usually, after ten minutes or so of discussion, I can see the light click on when the inventor realizes it is unrealistic to think he or she can compete with major game companies on a national level. At this point they become interested in what I have to say about planning a marketing program.

Strategic Plan

This is the big picture. At this level we are going to answer the question, "where is the product going to sell?"

Once you realize that only people listed in the Forbes 400 can afford to launch a game nationally, you are faced with deciding specifically where to launch/test market your product. The best way to accomplish this is to create a map of the United States composed of overlays, with each overlay providing a single piece of information.

Population. The first overlay should show the top twenty consumer markets in the United States. They should be coded so you can get a good idea of numerical size at a glance.

Tier One Retailers. The next overlay should identify the top twenty (ten would probably do) cities as far as numbers of Tier One Retailers. This information can be purchased, using mailing lists sorted by ZIP code. Once again, code the overlay's map so you can spot easily cities with significant concentrations.

Tier Two Retailers. Same as above.

Tier Three Retailers. Same as above.

Toys-R-Us. Same as above.

When these overlays are joined you can quickly see which cities contain population and game retail clusters. Other than Tier Three, Toys-R-Us, and a couple of statistical anomalies, the clusters will follow closely the population base. However, you need to do it anyway because you are going to start fine tuning to weed out cities as possible launch/test sites.

Depending upon the game's audience you will want to look for different characteristics in this weeding-out process. Of course there are many possibilities. Since we can only show one example, we will use an adult game which should appeal to college age people and older. Let's go a step further and say it is a social interactive game that could play well on radio or television commercials. Time to start adding overlays again.

CREATING A MARKET TEST MODEL

Universities. Our game appeals to the college crowd so it makes sense to launch it in a town with a large student population.

Radio Stations with "X" Market Share. A trip to the public library and a few hours in the Standard Rate and Data Directory (in many public libraries) should produce this list. The "X" market share you are looking for is based on the total percent of the potential listening audience as related to a station's actual listeners who fall within your game's demographics. For example, if our game were a country & western music trivia game we sure would not want to spend energy and money promoting it on a heavy metal station.

Television Stations. Even though we don't have much of a budget for TV advertising, we still might want to try something with the launch and it may be important in coming years to know this works.

Print Media. Make sure an overlay shows areas with excellent print media: newspapers, local magazine, free papers, college papers, etc. Whether we buy ads in these or not may be questionable but trying to get press coverage in them definitely is important.

"Apostles". The last overlay should show cities in which you have apostles: i.e., friends, relatives, partners—anyone and everyone who

can help you in any way. Code these as to how reliable, durable, and helpful each can be.

The Big Picture

When you bring all the overlays together it will only take a few minutes to eliminate all but four or five possible launch/test markets. Once you have reduced the candidates to this level you will have to ponder the pros and cons of each because we cannot afford to spread the available funds over four or five and still have any real impact.

Continuing with this hypothetical game, we will select two: San Francisco and Dallas. From a purely demographic point of view Chicago, Los Angeles, Minneapolis, San Diego, and Boston were superior but we chose these two markets for other reasons. Our company is based in Dallas. We have a lot of connections and friends there and feel we can pull some extra media coverage and conduct a lot more promotional events simply because we are physically there.

We chose San Francisco as our second test site for a number of reasons. Our game possesses unusually high appeal among college students and the Bay Area has a high density university population. The Bay Area has a denser than normal cluster of Tier One, Two, and Three retailers. And one of the project's active partners lives and has connections there.

Strategic Plan Outline

Our strategic outline might look like this:

YEAR ONE
    Product launch/test
        Dallas/Ft. Worth, Texas
        San Francisco Bay Area, California.

YEAR TWO
    Market Development
        Dallas/Ft. Worth
        San Francisco Bay Area
    Product launch
        Chicago
        San Diego
        Boston
        Minneapolis

YEAR THREE
    Market Development
        Dallas/Ft. Worth
        San Francisco
        Chicago
        San Diego
        Boston
        Minneapolis
    Product Launch
        Los Angeles
        Seattle
        Denver
        Detroit
        Philadelphia
        New York

Atlanta
Houston
San Antonio

Tactical Plan Now that we know where we are going to be selling this wonderful game, let's roll up our sleeves and figure out *how* we are going to sell them. After all, we are realistic enough to know those buyers are not sitting around asking, "When is that new game company from Dallas going to call about that game I have been waiting for?"

Remember, this is based on a hypothetical game and is only an example used to acquaint you with the process. We will discuss each element in more detail later. Following the plan that is about to unfold could work or be disastrous depending on a myriad of factors. To use a currently popular phrase—don't try this at home.

Hypothetical Plan MISSION STATEMENT

To achieve some Tier One Retail exposure nationally while creating maximum results in two markets, Dallas/Ft. Worth and San Francisco, using similar programs in each city.

STEP ONE: National Tier One Retail Exposure
  Trade Shows
      New York Toy Fair
      Dallas Toy Fair/Gift Show
      Pomona Toy Fair
      Game Manufacturers Las Vegas Game Show
  Trade Magazines (product release articles)
      Playthings
      Toy & Hobby World
      The Toy Book
      Games Magazine
  Direct Mail Program to Selected Tier One Retailers
  Telephone Sales Program to Selected Tier One Retailers

STEP TWO: Test Cities Sales and Promotions
  Tier One Retailers
      Armed with promotional and advertising program, sales force canvasses (physically if possible) key game retailers asking if they will be willing to participate in this product launch by allowing in-store game demonstrations and tournaments.
  Toys-R-Us and Tier Two Retailers
      Armed with strong promotional and advertising program sales force explains our company can not promote the game nationally but we will have a positive impact in our two target markets. Would the buyer be willing to run our product in the stores in these markets during the fourth quarter?
  Put P.R. campaign in place for fourth quarter execution
      Don't waste precious media coverage prematurely.
  Create Advertising Program
      Metropolitan print media
      One or two local radio stations
      College newspapers

Free papers

STEP THREE: (Execute fourth quarter product launch/test)

When a Plan Comes Together

Few happenings satisfy more than when the elements of a complex plan click into place. If everything in the above outline comes together perfectly, the following is a synopsis of what could happen.

You visit key game specialty retailers (preferably near college campuses) and explain the product launch program, inviting them to participate by allowing and promoting tournaments and demonstrations in their stores. You will take care of all the details; tables, games, prizes, promotional handouts, even an ad in the nearby college paper. All they have to do is provide space in the store and place one of the promotional handouts in each customer's shopping bag for thirty days before the event.

You will even bring extra reserve stock in the day of the event so the merchant will have no fear of running out or of buying too much. Of course, it's a good idea for the merchant to stock a few games before the tournament in case someone wants to practice. Be sure to make it clear to the merchant—repeating it for emphasis—that he has nothing to lose. After the merchant agrees to participate, send him a follow-up letter with the conditions, dates and expectations stated clearly. That way there should be no confusion.

Once you have set up a number of these programs at stores near college campuses, approach other Tier One specialty retailers—key area game stores not necessarily near colleges. Offer the same deal to them except provide in-store demonstrations rather than tournaments. Shoppers often don't want to spend the time to play a game though they will spend a moment or two to listen to a game's concept and (if you can explain this part in under a minute) how it works. Never read or ask anyone to read your rules during a demonstration.

When you have all these events scheduled, meet with the local department store buyers and explain your advertising and demonstration promotion program. Offer to provide autograph or demonstration sessions if they will agree to stock your game during the product test.

When you have as many in-store events booked as you can handle (some will cancel at the last minute), begin a sales campaign to alert every other merchant in the test market area who sells games. This should consist of personal visits (by appointment only) from you or your rep, telemarketing, and direct mail programs. Tell them they are located in your product launch area, and describe your advertising, promotion, and public relations program. (This program begins as a budget and a plan and evolves along with the sales program.)

Toys-R-Us and Tier Two retailers should be contacted with a detailed explanation of the program. Try to get them to stock your game, but only in the test city.

During this time, you will feel swamped with details, overwhelmed with work, and short of hours and manpower. Good. That means you are off to a good start.

As selling and arranging in-store demonstrations progresses so will the rest of your advertising and promotion programs.

You have selected three or four radio stations as candidates to carry commercials. Get together with their sales representatives. Explain that your game will play very well on the air and you think radio commercials should be an effective way to advertise. Tell them your budget will allow you to buy time on one or two stations only, so ask them to put together a proposal for you; one that shows how much it would cost to have them produce your 30 second spot and run it during good air time.

Send a follow-up letter, thanking them for their time and telling them that it occurred to you that it would be fun for the listeners if, as part of the radio ad campaign, you visited with disk jockeys a couple of times a week and played the game on the air. You, of course, would be delighted to provide prizes. As an afterthought you might mention that you know some announcers are opposed to having guests and that you would be just as happy if they would play the game on the air themselves. Once you have locked up one or two radio stations with both ads and free air time, incorporate these details into your promotional campaign. In, fact, if you have enough commercial time you can offer to add a tag line (something like "This game is available at X,Y,Z Department Store") when a store buys a large quantity of games.

Publicity in the Print and Broadcast Media

A local public relations company can be extremely helpful in getting you print coverage in this area, as well as in the next. If you feel you can afford PR help, look for a small operation—maybe a one-man or woman shop—who will work within your budget. If your budget is such that you have to choose between print or air time PR coverage, choose the print coverage.

Visit with the ad sales people for any magazines and newspapers you feel might help promote the product. Explain your situation again. You cannot afford all of them and want to make sure you spend your limited budget in the most effective manner possible. In your follow-up letter let them know editorial coverage would be greatly appreciated and that you believe their readers would be very interested. When your ads are completed and scheduled, include this in your promotion kit as well.

Organizations—Another Publicity Medium

Next, call on all the social organizations which might be interested in having you conduct teach-and-play tournaments. Examples would be fraternities, sororities, church social groups, singles clubs, and retirement centers; i.e., any place where large numbers of people congregate and where they welcome entertainment in almost any form. Book these events so they do not interfere with your in-store programs. If you can afford it, this might be the time and place to hire a temporary assistant; someone with quick intelligence, personal charm, and boundless enthusiasm. You might find a great part-timer who is willing to be paid by the event. If this person turns out to be really capable, you could use him or her to expand your in-store programs as well. When the entire schedule has been completed, unleash the PR efforts. Whether it is a public relations firm or your own in-house efforts, use direct mail and telephone to contact every magazine, newspaper, radio station, and television station in the area. Make them aware of your presence. Involve all the local merchants, social groups, and other organizations. The objective is to create as many articles and interviews as possible. Media events tend to feed off themselves. Once you get one interview it seems easier to get the next. Make sure to maintain a current press kit to keep reminding local media of the news story they might be missing.

When the big day comes (and if everything works), the program kicks off and slowly gains momentum through the fourth quarter, to the point that your game is a hot item from Thanksgiving to Christmas. Your sales, promotion, and advertising programs work effectively in unison, creating a successful product launch. That is marketing at its best.

If this just sounds to you like so much common sense any first-timer would use to launch a product, you are in the minority. Most people *do not have a clue* as to how to launch a new game. Having been exposed to over two hundred games in the last twenty years I have picked up a few pointers about success and failures and have some valuable opinions on what works and what doesn't.

There was a time when I was younger that I knew a lot less than I thought—and I did not have someone with 20 years experience at my shoulder to tell me what to do.

The Author's First Game ... A Learning Experience

When I did my first game I was so suffused with my own ego and so delighted at seeing my gem in print, to give even a passing thought to marketing. I was happy and relaxed, comforted by the belief that if a better mousetrap was built (which I felt I had done), people automatically would beat a path to my door. It never occurred to me that all the work I had put into designing the game and nursing the project through its various stages was just the beginning; a minor effort compared to the task of getting and keeping my game on the market.

My plans were quite sketchy, almost nonexistent in fact. Fortunately I had lived a clean life and providence came to my rescue. It must have! Based on everything I have learned since those early days, nothing but Divine Intervention could be credited with saving me from total ruin.

My first game went against all the rules. I produced only a thousand copies, creating a cost per unit that prohibited the game from being competitive in stores. This reality check limited me to the direct mail market. The theme of the game was an obscure campaign from the American Civil War, which meant I was creating a limited interest item in a narrow market. I titled it, "The Seven Days' Battles", an idea that came to me within three seconds after the artist asked me what to put on the box. The box art itself was a bland mix of a black line drawing from a hundred-year-old magazine and an undistinguished cream colored background. In short, everything was wrong with the game. I just did not realize it at the time.

I know now that I did it the hard way—managing and coordinating each component. Consequently, the printed box top label did not fit properly on the box top, the game board was just a hair too large for the box bottom, about a quarter of the die-cutting had to be thrown out because I had not left enough tolerance, and the bargain dice I bought tended to soften and melt in temperatures over 80 degrees. I didn't falter, though. It was still a good product and soon, very soon, I knew people would be flocking to my garage door to find a copy of this game about which they had heard so much.

Being too impatient to wait for the first printed copies I took a photograph of my prototype and made up a quarter page ad, which I sent along with a check to the *Civil War Times Illustrated* magazine. Because of the long lead time the ad did not appear for three months, but —as things turned out—this was for the best. The boxes, boards, and playing pieces, which were being made by three different vendors, were completed almost three months late. They wound up being delivered two days after I received my copy of the magazine, with the advertisement buried 90 pages into it.

I began assembling games frantically and packed them for mailing. When orders started arriving I was elated. Every day I went to the post office, picked up ten or more envelopes containing checks, went back home and shipped these wise people their games. I had other ads scheduled to appear in various other magazines, but none of them were out yet. Anticipating seemingly endless sales—based on the fact that I had sold nearly 400 copies through one ad alone—I seriously contemplated ordering reprints.

When the other ads finally started appearing, the orders fell far short of my expectations. In fact, they fell far short of reaching the lowest level of my worst fears. The reason for this, I discovered later, was that what I was now getting is considered average response to mail order ads. My first ad had pulled enormous results for one reason—blind luck. The issue of *Civil War Times Illustrated* in which it appeared had carried several lengthy articles on the Seven Days' Battles campaign. My orders resulted from the interest created by those articles.

Had it not been for this monumental stroke of luck, it's likely I never would have entered the game business. As it turned out, fate took a hand. I had done nearly everything wrong (though at the time I would have told anyone how brilliant I was), paid virtually no attention to the advice I received, and still managed to break into the business.

Since those shaky early days I have come to the realization that the key to success is marketing. I have seen brilliant games, produced by individuals or small companies, come into the market and vanish without a trace. Why? They probably believed as I did, that making the game was the big job and that the sales would take care of themselves. I have seen a most mediocre game, one produced by a persistent marketer, carve out a permanent niche in the marketplace simply because he knew how and where to sell his game.

PRICING

Before setting about to market a game, you must set its selling price. In order to do this, you first must determine how much it is going to cost to produce. This requires two pieces of information: precise specifications for the game's components and the number of games you will be manufacturing. Let's get an idea of what we are dealing with by taking a hypothetical game from start to finish. Our scenario involves a fairly recent development in the game market.

The popularity of home video and computer games made a major impact on the sales of board games. At first the impact was negative. Everyone was spending their money on the cute little games with illuminated monsters eating their way across a screen. As the novelty wore off, people returned to more traditional games. When video games were the rage they were not cheap, with some costing as much as

$40.00. This raised the perceived value of board games in the eyes of consumers. Before the computer games fad, game manufacturers believed a price barrier existed; i.e., no game would sell in the mass market for more than $10.00. Today, as substantiated by the likes of *Trivial Pursuit*, a well-made, high quality board game can sell for as much as a video game. The only catch is that the board game *must* be top quality, with the kind of packaging and presentation that enables it to sell as a gift item.

Let's get back to our hypothetical game and look at that beauty. Good looking game board! Great looking box! Say, this art is pretty good, too! Now, all the art and typesetting winds up costing at least $3,000. (If your game is a trivia or information-driven game, the typesetting cost will be considerably higher—unless you can do it yourself on a computer.) Figure on another $3,000 for the four-color separations and $1,500 for the stripping (to get everything ready to be put on the press), and it looks like an initial investment of $7,500 without a single copy in sight.

These are the set-up or prep charges. Some game companies amortize them over the initial print run, others spread them out over many more copies than are first printed, and still others don't amortize them at all, instead carrying them on their books as an asset. To get a realistic picture of what the game will actually cost to produce it's best to include these prep charges in the initial print run, which makes the initial run a million dollar question.

Make too many of these things and you could wind up eating them with ketchup. Make too few and the cost per game is going to be so high that the game won't be marketable. This is a big decision, one on which your basic marketing strategy will hinge, so the future of your gaming empire is already at stake. Don't panic, though. Simply ask the printer for a quote on 2,500, 5,000, 10,000 and 25,000 copies, with a reprint price for 25,000.

How can I advise you so glibly? Simple! All that is really required is a quote on four quantities for the initial run and a quote for reprints, to eliminate any prep or set-up charges the second time around.

Unless you have an angel or have had a recent windfall, you probably are not going to be able to afford more than 10,000 copies of the game. And unless you are testing in more than two major markets you do not need more than this. At this level we are talking a minimum investment of $70,000, and that's assuming the game is pretty basic. Going down the scale, 5,000 copies of the game should cost $55,000, which would push the retail price up a bit. At the bottom of the barrel, 2,500 copies will cost somewhere around $37,000. If you are going to try to wholesale the game to retailers, it will be difficult to eke out a worthwhile profit out of so small a run. So why would anyone bother producing this minimal quantity? They do it because of the options involved.

If you are test marketing in only one city and have a limited promotion budget, there is no point in making more than you need. Especially when you realize the product likely will be changed as a result of the test marketing.

Below is a chart showing how many games to produce for a market test in some cities based on modest promotion budgets. **WARNING:** These figures are based on you working around the clock to make the launch successful. They reflect the best results some successful clients achieved after they had invested enormous amounts of creativity, persistence, and energy. There is no guarantee you will do this well. There is also no straight population curve because sales in these cities are affected by all the things discussed in creating your overlay marketing map.

GAME	CITY	BUDGET	UNITS SOLD
Quick Wit	Chicago	$6,000	5,500
Notable Quotables	San Diego	$5,000	4,000
Uncommon Sense	Dallas	$2,000	900
Clever Endeavor	Chicago	$7,500	7,000
U.S.A. Trivia	San Francisco	$4,000	3,000
Earth Alert	Seattle	$2,500	1,000

Remember that your own sales will vary significantly, depending upon your marketing effectiveness.

Let's assume the test market requires 5,000 units. We will assign a retail price to the item high enough to recover as much of the cost and expenses as possible, yet low enough to be acceptable to interested consumers. To go about this, we determine the raw cost per unit. In this case, it's $12.50 per game, if we include the $7,500 spent on art work, putting us near the wholesale price of some mass market competing products.

With this kind of cost, we have to look on the limited run as a "market test." We are going to try to sell out as quickly as possible and hope to break even. There just is no way to wholesale (selling to stores and distributors who in turn retail to consumers) at this level and make a profit. This is because the price must be structured so as to allow the retailers to make a profit.

I could have said fair profit, but if you are in the situation we're discussing, you won't think there is anything fair about it. This means having a suggested retail price of $29.95 per game, about right for a social interactive adult mass-market game, (Some recent entries into this market have met limited success at retail price points of $34.95 and even $39.95.) When you wholesale the game, it will sell to stores at 50% off the retail price, $14.98, plus freight charges. Almost all firms buying games get at least 50% off and 30 days in which to pay the bill. If they buy a large enough quantity, they usually get freight paid as well.

The Question of Profitability

Let's stop and think about where we are at this point. We have 5,000 games to sell at $14.98 apiece. Being super salespeople with a first class product launch plan, we manage to do this quickly and the last items are shipped out 90 days after we've received them. Tack on another 30 days to collect all the money and estimate that about 10% of our customers are going to be late in paying (if at all), and we can anticipate a gross sales of $74,900.

Not bad for 5,000 copies, you may say, but now we have to start deducting. We said about 10% of the debt would not be collected on time and maybe never, so subtract $7,500. Then subtract the marketing expenses that made the test successful, another $5,000. There is also the $3,000 for the sales flyer and another $1,500 for the mailing list and postage to mail it to all the specialty game shops in the country. Travel and accommodations for you to be in the target market during the product launch—an absolute minimum of $60.00 per day plus transportation—add up to another $2,500. You incurred about $1,000 in long distance phone call expense. For general business correspondence stationery, envelopes, and postage) add another $500. There were probably some other expenses not identified here, but what we have will be enough to make a point.

+$ 74,900.00	gross sales
-$ 7,500.00	for late payment or bad debts
-$ 5,000.00	product launch budget
-$ 4,500.00	sales flyer, list & mail
-$ 2,500.00	travel expenses
-$ 1,000.00	telephone
-$ 500.00	office supply expenses
+$ 53,900.00	gross profit.

Now subtract the $62,500.00 in product costs—the games, art, and negatives—and you can begin to understand the concept of deficit spending; $8,600 in deficit spending.

You may be able to do a little better than this by shaving a nickel here, maybe staying with a friend or relative in the test market area. However, notice there is absolutely no overhead figured into this. No money to pay neighborhood kids to ship items. No mention of rental for warehouse space, utilities, or transportation of the items from the printer's facilities to our own. These are all details requiring ingenuity, some child labor and a spouse's willingness to let you get this idea out of our system. In addition, we have not figured on funds for trade shows and conventions. So why are we bothering to do only 5,000 copies?

Options ... What Next?   This small run offers a couple of options. The first is being able to test the waters. At the end of the market test we will see how difficult it will be to sell out a small quantity and how long it will take. We also will learn which stores are likely to come back for reorders. But, you say, we have done all this work and sold all these games and we still have just about the same amount of money with which we started. What's the big deal?

It's time to put things in perspective. We only had to sell 5,000 copies, not 10,000 or 25,000. If it took us that much effort and money to sell the smaller quantity, how would it feel knowing there were still 20,000 to go? Having sold the games, tested the market, recovered some of the investment, and *learned a lot*, we can go on from there.

If we are satisfied with the game's reception; i.e., everybody reordered within a week, sold out within a month, and making money was never so easy, then we know we should reprint the game and keep it on the market. After this experience we can gauge how many will be sold in a month and how many to reprint to start making a profit. It's important to keep a cool head, however, and not let rampant enthusiasm take over; printing 100,000 copies, for example, and hiring scores of salespeople. Increase the print run from the initial 5,000 to between 10,000 and 25,000 copies this time around. That gives us some room to work out a more acceptable price/profit ratio, but does not threaten to leave us with warehouses full of inventory if the sales growth curve heads south.

TIME TO APPROACH THE BIG GAME COMPANIES?

Let's assume things went okay; not great, but pretty well. All 5,000 copies sold but it took a lot longer than expected. If you decide to reprint 10-25,000 copies and keep plugging away in the market place, we will want to factor in some profit for your time and effort. Suppose we did all right, but decide it just is not worth the effort to continue. But we do have a published game that did sell, and this affords us yet another option: approaching big game companies.

That's right! Those same companies that would not even open our letters before may look at the game now because they won't be looking at just a concept. They are going to be looking at a published game, along with a marketing analysis covering sales on the first 5,000 units over a six-month period. They are not going to worry about being sued for copyright infringement because the game already has been published and copyrighted. Consequently, they do not even have to worry about somebody filing a harassment suit in case the game is similar to their own.

If we send a crisp, professional letter and follow up with a phone call or two, we should be able to persuade someone to at least look at the game. If they make an offer to buy the rights to it, we know we gave it our best shot and now can look forward to earning royalties while someone else takes over responsibility for sales.

REPRINT POSSIBILITIES

The options obtained by producing only 5,000 copies should appeal to the pessimist in us. What about the other quantities, 10,000 or 25,000? They offer the same options but with the added disadvantage of taking longer to sell out. To compensate for the longer selling period, they offer some advantages that could not be factored into the smaller run.

Let's take the 10,000 quantity first. We already have established a hypothetical cost of $7 per game at this level, and we will maintain a retail price of $29.95. At this price we still get $14.98 each from retailers, but have room to pay freight costs if a buyer orders high volume. We also have room for more sales expenses, so we can run an extra ad or two.

We know that since we have twice as many units, it's going to take us longer to move the games, but we hope not twice as long. After all, our marketing plan should have all the major wrinkles ironed out by now and any added time means additional sales expense.

10,000 copies at $7 each (you absorbed the cost of the art and negatives in the first run) is $70,000 for the COG (cost of goods). Our expenditures will be as follows:

ITEM	AMOUNT
Marketing (promotion, advertising, trade shows)	$30,000
Sale Commissions (reps at 10% of 14.98 per unit)	14,500
Freight ($.50 per game for 5,000 games)	2,500
Travel (trade shows, sales and promotions)	7,500
Bad Debt (based on 5% of sales)	7,500
Operating expenses (phone, fax, etc.)	3,500
TOTAL	$65,500

Add in a COG of $70,000 and the total cost comes to $135,500. How did we do? We sold 10,000 copies at $14.98 each; gross sales figure of $149,800 and a net profit of $14,300. The problem is that we included no salaries in our expenses. If you are asking "how am I suppose to make a living from this?" the answer is, you're not. It's time for another reality check.

When Milton Bradley commits to manufacture a game, they are not looking at 10,000 or even 100,000 units. They produce a minimum of 250,000 units. They are gaining major economies of scale that simply are not available to you. From the standpoint of profit, you cannot expect to compete with these companies when you make 5-10,000 copies at a time. Similarly it is unreasonable to expect to make a living, or earn a satisfactory return on your investment, from market tests. To make any money in the game business you must be selling a minimum of 25,000 pieces annually on a national basis without disproportionate sales costs.

If you decide on a second run, you will have to take care not to over-extend yourself. The game market is a fickle place and it's important to remember, it takes about four years for the average game to reach a true market position. This means a four-year commitment on your part.

CONSUMER ADVERTISING

Consumer advertising is dangerous and expensive. It is dangerous if it works before you have broad product distribution. Why? Because you are spending money and creativity motivating people to seek a hard to find product. Think of yourself. How many places will you look for a new product in which you are casually interested before saying it's not worth the effort? Not many. Advertising is expensive even when it works; very expensive when it does not. If it fails either because you did not have adequate distribution or because the ad itself was bad, placed in the wrong medium or at the wrong time, it can be devastatingly expensive.

If you are doing consumer advertising to support product in a specific market (city or region) try to concentrate on the lowest cost per thousand (CPM) vehicle that reaches your highest potential audience. If your game appeals to college kids, college newspapers are a sound choice. They are relatively low cost and they are read by exactly the right audience. But just as you would not advertise a preschool game in a college paper, it does not make sense to advertise a game for college students in an expensive metropolitan newspaper—unless you are certain a majority of college kids read it. Research in the Standard Rate and Data Directory at the public library will help you match targeted audience with appropriate magazines and newspapers.

1-800-The Game In the last twenty years 800 number television ads have exploded as a new marketing technique. Unbreakable ginsu knives, Slim Whitman records, windshield wipers, and other unusual items have made a number of entrepreneurs millionaires. Does it work for games? I know three clients who can tell you it did not work for them.

A few years ago, when television wrestling shows were hugely popular, an enterprising young businessman came to me and said, "Look, I don't know anything about games but I have a connection with this television wrestling firm that is syndicated into over one hundred cities and..." His plan was to make a relatively inexpensive game, promote it with an 800 number, and make a bundle while television wrestling was at its popularity peak. Initially, to make the greatest profit, he wanted to manufacture 100,000 copies. I tried to convince him to do 25,000 initially. He compromised on 50,000.

While we were making the games, he acquired many TV spots, with air time before, during, and after this particular wrestling program. He produced a good commercial and started selling the product to retailers. When the commercials aired he literally held his breath waiting for the phones to start ringing. They didn't, and the commercials were pulled after two weeks. They were not generating orders. Being a good businessman, he knew when to cut his losses, no matter how substantial they were.

What has 32 teeth and an IQ of 248? Give up? The first six rows of spectators at a wrestling match. Anyway, that's one 800 number marketing failure. Here's another . . .

A Certified Public Accountant invented a trivia game based on the Bible. For months he studied his game, the market, his plans, costs, customer demographics, and just about everything else you might imagine. He had seen a number of businesses fail and was a cautious, conservative investor. He wanted to make sure he had at least a reasonable chance of success before plunking down his money. When he finally committed to the project, he chose to market the game through churches and via an 800 number television advertising campaign. He produced an excellent commercial and bought spots on Christian cable channels.

Disaster struck. Orders materialized, but not nearly enough to cover the cost of the air time or the cost of the product. The accountant was stunned. He had spent months studying and planning. Even in his worst "What if?" scenarios the ads should not have pulled so poorly.

Another client flew in from Manhattan. He has spent an impressive number of years as a marketer in the rock & roll music industry. He showed me his market research book. It must have weighed ten pounds and contained hundreds of pages of statistics and customer demographics. His idea was to make a game based on the rock & roll industry and promote it through 800 number ads on MTV and VH1 (the music video cable channels). The computer analysis of his research material indicated that it would be virtually impossible for him to execute his plan and sell less than 15,000 games from November 1 until December 10.

The ads were pulled after two weeks. Another huge disappointment. What has 32 teeth and an IQ of 248? The first six spectator rows at a rock concert.

No one really knows why 800 numbers have not worked well for games, but I have a theory. I think adults who play games tend to read more and watch television less than the rest of the country. If this is true, 800 number commercials on late night network television or obscure cable channels reach people who read less and don't play games much. They are counter productive because the subject of the ads does not match the interests of the audience.

I will finish this 800 number dissertation on a brighter note. Another client produced a game based on crossword puzzles. He was having a difficult time selling it to retailers when he stumbled onto a television shopping club — one of those channels that parades merchandise across the screen, screaming at you to buy it now! Now! **NOW!** They tried it and did all right. But then they came up with the idea of playing it on the air every day for twenty minutes; like a television game show except the contestants would call in. It was a great success. My client sold them nearly 40,000 games before the show played out.

If you are dead set on trying 800 number advertising, don't do it yourself. There are many established companies that know how to make it work. If your product is right for it, they will buy it from you and run the commercials themselves.

Print Advertising

Do you think that you are going to sell your product through direct mail, get the full retail price, and make a great profit on a short run? It sounds great, but it seldom works. The more realistic position is that you are going to run some print media ads to support your marketing. The ads will offer readers shopping by direct mail. In effect, any money generated by those sales will be subsidizing the cost of the ad. You should think of it this way because there is an enormous difference between being in the direct mail business and selling one item by direct mail.

Prospecting by Direct Mail

When you are in the direct mail business you look for customers by offering products in specialty magazines. It is called prospecting and it is not uncommon for each customer who responds to a magazine ad to end up costing the company $4-6.00. However, it is worth it to a direct mail company. They now have the name of a person who responded to their ad for a plastic model of a World War II tank, and can assume that person is likely to be interested in models, tanks, World War II, and military history in general.

When that model tank arrives in the customer's mail, you can be sure it will be accompanied by a handful of special offers; items the company thinks the new customer will find interesting. A month later he begins receiving their regular mailings. The next time he buys the company makes a profit.

When you sell your game by direct mail, your prospecting costs are no different than for any other business. The difference is that you do not have any follow-up products to offset the initial cost of reaching your customer.

I am not saying you never should use direct mail ads. I am saying you should not put all your eggs in this one basket. If your budget is so limited as to restrict you to this form of marketing, try what I suggested to a lady with a game based on a crossword puzzle.

She was a soft-spoken, determined woman. She was from the country, so had very little of the big city slickness that prevents many people from really listening and taking advice. She showed me her prototype and was genuinely interested in
turing specifications and packaging. She paid attention, making notes of even negative comments. Halfway through listing half a dozen sound reasons why she should not make a game based on this theme, I realized she was going to anyway.

Her original plan was to sell it by direct mail through ads in crossword puzzle magazines. These tend to have substantial circulations and relatively low cost per thousand costs. I suggested she not manufacture any games. Instead, have an artist make a great prototype, photograph it for the ad, and then run the ads in the appropriate magazines. If enough people ordered, the art and film would be ready and enable her to get into production immediately. If not enough people ordered, she could return their money and apologize, advising prospective buyers she did not get enough responses to warrant manufacturing the product.

Because she had a very limited budget she saw the wisdom of this approach and set the plan in motion. Several months later, when the magazine ads had been out for 60 days and had generated about that many orders, she called to thank me for saving her tens of thousands of dollars.

Do-It-Yourself Advertising

If you are going to run print ads, find out as much as you can about the publications before charting your course. After you have acquainted yourself with the names, addresses, and advertising rates for special interest magazines appropriate to your game, prepare your ad(s) and start scheduling them to appear after your game is ready to be shipped. Don't get too anxious. It is very important that the ads not appear before the games are ready.

If possible, fill the orders the same day they arrive. You will want your customers to think that you and your company have it all together. This may seem a little exaggerated, but it isn't. I have seen too many people turned off by having to wait for mail order items. By the time the order is filled — often a number of weeks later—the customer has lost whatever interest he had in the first place.

Spend a lot of time creating your ads. Regardless of the size of the advertisement, the headline has to grab the reader's attention. If it does not, I can almost guarantee you the rest of the ad copy won't be read. Look through some magazines for headlines, then cut out the ads and accumulate a bunch of them. Sort through them, making stacks of best, good, and the "why did you pick them in the first place" categories. Take notes on the best of the best and try to determine whether there is a possible tie-in with your own product. When you're finished you will have a pretty good idea of how to make your own ad work.

Once you have the headline, do a sketch of an accompanying photograph of your game all laid out, with the box standing up behind the board and components. Then get started on the copy. Make it honest and upbeat and remember—you are doing it with pencil and paper, not chisel and stone. Don't be afraid to make changes. Touch on what you think people will want to know about the game; e.g., what it's about, is it easy to learn, who it's geared for. Since the ad copy has to sell the game in much the same way as the box back copy, you may be able to use some of the same written material.

As is true of just about everything else in life, there are right ways and wrong ways to write ad copy. One wrong way is to say something like, "This game is about football. It's a lot of fun because people who like football will enjoy it. It's easy to learn and easy to play and everyone will want to. It sells for $29 and you can order it from the address below."

This little recitation answers all the questions, but it falls short in creating enthusiasm or desire. Let's try it again, but with a little more "sizzle" this time.

"The score is tied. The two-minute warning seems a lifetime ago. It's third down and six, your last chance to get in field goal range. The ball is snapped. The quarterback fades back as the defenders blitz. He side-steps one tackler, ducks under another, firing a long pass down the sideline. The receiver leaps to make the catch only to be hit on his way down. He bobbles the ball, holds on, breaks a tackle, and heads down field. He's at the 50, the 40, the 35, he's. . . .

You'll experience the excitement of professional football when you play. . .JOCKO.

JOCKO! It's a new game for the armchair coach in all of us. Easy to learn and fast-paced to play, JOCKO creates the feeling of being on the gridiron as YOU make the decisions and YOU call the plays. No longer will you have to watch passively as your favorite team struggles against its arch rivals. In less time than it takes to watch a game, you'll actually play it. JOCKO! A great game for the whole family. It's available at better stores everywhere. Ask for it or order directly from us. This exciting new board game is yours for only $29. So come on, get out of those bleachers and onto the field. Place your order today."

This may not be perfect but it is a whole lot better than the first attempt. It represents only one type of approach. Once you have looked through a ton of magazines, you'll find many possible styles.

After settling on your ad and neatly typing it and marking it for headlines, in bold and italic type, make another run to the artist. He probably will have to make some changes, because people generally write more copy than will fit comfortably in an ad. Then you will have to do a rewrite. As long as the copy is being rewritten anyway, save yourself some time by instructing the artist to lay out the ad to run in full, half and quarter-page sizes. It's a sure bet you will not be able to afford a full page ad in every publication you have chosen, but you should try to get as much mileage out of the typesetting as possible. Tell the artist how many copies of each size you will need, so that everything will be ready to be picked up at once.

Advertising to the Trade

Once they have been mailed, forget about the consumer publication ads for a month or two, until they begin to appear. Start concentrating on a different ad, this one for trade publications. These are magazines written for people in a particular business or occupation; in this case, retailers and wholesalers. There are actually quite a few and their names and addresses can be found in directories at local libraries, or by asking toy and game merchants for back issues. Before starting to work on an ad for this group, you should try to understand how these people think.

First, trade people buy and sell a lot of games. Hundreds of titles are thrown at them every year. They don't have the time or the inclination to study every one of them. If a game looks to be a big seller, they will know about it before anybody else. If a game is a real dog, they'll know that too. But if a game is new and does not have a track record, they tend to base their decisions on the following factors: how does the package look? Will it attract attention and make people want to pick it up? Will the back of the box sell the game? How much promotion/advertising is behind it? What are the discounts and terms, and is there enough profit involved to make it worth handling? By now you know this routine . . .

Notice there is no mention of whether the game is fun to play or who is going to play it. These people are not game playing experts; they are merchants. They are interested only in how fast they can sell this merchandise and how much money they will make in the process.

An advertisement that is fighting to gain attention in the trade publications must address specific marketing needs. It requires more pictures, less text. The copy should emphasize promotion, discounts, packaging, and the game's ability to sell itself. If you have placed ads in a well-known magazine, add a line saying, "As seen in *Big Time Magazine*", to create the impression the game is supported by a lot of advertising.

Considering the cost of advertising, this impression will be only an illusion. When major companies promote a game, they may spend several million dollars, but they do it for reasons other than one might expect.

The first time I witnessed this technique was at a trade show in Atlanta. There I was in my plain, cheaply outfitted ten-by-ten-foot booth, sitting across from the elaborate booth of an internationally known toy company. Talk about something deflating your ego! Their exhibit was worth more than my entire company. Anyway, they had an item, kind of a plastic tricycle for preschoolers, toy buyers were lining up to order. At one point the line was so long it extended beyond their area and bumped into mine. Quite a few of the buyers glanced at my limited line of wares without much interest while they waited to place orders for the hot tricycle.

I struck up a conversation with one particularly friendly gentleman. He was kind enough to show me how advertising could work in the toy and game industry. It seemed this particular toy manufacturer had budgeted around three million dollars to promote his product on television during the coming Christmas season. The company had a big chart showing which stations would air the commercials and in what cities. As a special favor to the retailers that bought in large enough quantities, the manufacturer would let them plug their stores at the end of the commercials. You see this kind of thing all the time. A commercial comes on showing shapely young women drinking soda in an island setting and at the end a sign flashes on the screen saying, "Available at Ripo Supermarkets".

Loss Leaders

These buyers actually were waiting in line to place hundreds of thousands of dollars in orders, and the man I'm talking to is telling me why it's such a good deal! The toy manufacturer is selling an item for $14 the stores will sell to customers for $13.95—and this is a good deal? This means the stores lose five cents on each item sold, doesn't it? What's going on here?

It's called a *loss leader*. The store owner buys the item for slightly more than he sells it because the manufacturer's advertising attracts people to his store. He is gambling that once these customers are in the store, they will purchase something other than the advertised product.

Can you compete with that? Of course not, unless your game is so popular and in such demand that people are clamoring for it. Be grateful that the major manufacturers usually do this with only one item during the holiday selling season.

Loss leaders are not just a phenomenon of the games and toys business. Virtually all producers of consumer items who can afford to commit the advertising dollars do it every now and then, sometimes as a means of selling down their stock of slower moving items. Fortunately they will not affect you too much, since you will not be selling to very many major outlets in the beginning.

Back to the trade ads. Most trade magazines charge more for advertising space than might be expected, based on their circulation. There is a simple reason for this. They are offering to send their magazine containing your ad to known buyers of a product category and their only real income is from the sale of advertising space. In many cases the magazine is free to qualified subscribers.

The people who sell space for these publications do only that. They are hustlers (not in any dishonest sense) who work hard to earn a living. Once they find out someone is a prospective buyer of advertising space, they can be relentless. Don't be persuaded to advertise in one publication only. Make it clear you have a limited budget, all of which has been committed. Tell them you will get back with them, based on the performance of the current series of ads. Don't be shy. They aren't.

TRADE PUBLICATIONS: NEW PRODUCT SECTIONS

In addition to carrying advertising and having other regular news and information features, trade publications also have "New Products" sections. This section, usually photo-illustrated, spotlights new items of interest to buyers. Send a copy of your game to the magazine for inclusion in this section and you will receive what is, in effect, free advertising space. You will be able to show a picture of the box top, a line or two about the game, the name and address of your company, the suggested retail price and, in some cases, a reader service number.

When they are used, reader service numbers are seen throughout the magazine at the foot of ads and new product announcements. There is a postage-paid response card—often called a "bingo card"—in the back of the publication the reader can tear out, fill in, and mail to obtain additional information. You receive a computerized printout with all this data, including the names and addresses of the companies who circled your number. You follow up these leads in an effort to create new customers.

This is a good service. If you are going to promote your game in trade publications, you should take advantage of both the free publicity available in the new product section and the sales leads generated by the reader service card.

THE CIRCUIT— GET OUT AND SELL

For five years, Gary Gygax travelled around the country in a beat-up Volkswagen microbus promoting *DUNGEONS & DRAGONS.* Gary Gabriel sold *Pente* out of the back of his van and at flea markets for three and a half years. For four years, Hazel Bowman wound her motor home along Sunbelt highways and byways peddling *Skip-Bo.* When you find a successful game you are almost certain to find behind it a story filled with hard work, dedication, and a long-term promotional effort.

It makes sense to tie in these promotion loops or circuits with your travels to and from product launch target markets. Never pass up an opportunity to sell your game to a small town gift store or to teach a waitress at a roadside cafe how to play.

After the ads have been placed and the games warehoused it's time to get out there and push the product. Everyone else with a game on the market is sweating right alongside you to ensure that their product sells. You cannot afford to be different. I hope you enjoy traveling, because you are in for a lot of it.

Do Not Ignore the Board Game Conventions

Your starting-off point may be one of the numerous board game conventions that are held for consumers. These tend to be small and are scattered around the country at different times during the year. Nearly all trade and game specialty magazines publish monthly calendars of all the major conventions as well as some minor ones. If your game fits the product category, it's important to attend as many of these shows as possible during the first year of your game's life. This is an important place to get your word-of-mouth advertising started.

The people who attend these conventions are hard core gamers. If they like a game and buy it, they will start teaching their friends as soon as they get home. True, most of these conventions have a fantasy, science-fiction or military history theme, but I have seen major corporations in attendance more than once. Even such giants as Parker Brothers and Milton Bradley occasionally take booths.

Go to these conventions with two objectives in mind: to demonstrate and to sell. To demonstrate the game try running mini-tournaments, teaching the rules before each round. Copies of the game will serve as prizes. Be your most charming and personable, doing your best to get people really excited. Get them whooping and hollering over each throw of the dice. This draws a crowd, which is exactly what you want. The more people who actually look at the game, the more you will have a chance to sell.

You should try to sell at least a few copies while at these conventions, not only to promote word-of-mouth advertising but also to help defray travel costs. Most of the time you will be able to rent booth space and tables for a reasonable charge. If you can't recruit some free help, divide your time between selling and running demonstrations. After a few of these exhibitions you are going to get really bored, and you will find yourself coming up with excuses for not attending any more shows. You *must* persevere. Conventions are the most concentrated way to show your game to lots of people.

IN-STORE DEMONSTRATIONS

I remember a game we produced a few years ago. It was a role playing game and we were taking it into an over-saturated market against strong, well-entrenched competition. We had a promotions man, sort of like the old Duncan Yo-Yo men of years past, who travelled around the country doing demonstrations in stores. I foolishly volunteered to travel with him for a few weeks, helping out with demonstrations. Each display involved running an adventure or scenario for four to ten players. Each episode lasted about three hours, unless the kids were really into it and were having fun. Then it could run up to four or five hours.

But it was *always* the same adventure. By the third time I had done it, I knew fifty pages of the text by heart. By the tenth time I did not even bother to take out the book. By the 20th time I could do it while catching forty winks. I ran the same adventure nearly 200 times in about half as many days and I was so sick of it at the end of the tour I wanted to burn all my personal copies of the game. But you know something? It worked!

When we looked at the sales statistics a year later, we found that the game did better in the states where I did the demos than in the states I had not visited. Taking the time to demonstrate the game to 1,000 people sold an additional 5,000 copies that first year. Don't minimize the usefulness of demos. They are a powerful tool. Once you feel comfortable with them, you will find the results of your efforts reflected in your sales.

Why are in-store demonstrations so effective? There are a couple of reasons. The obvious one is that it gets consumers playing the game without having to read the rules. The people who win your tournaments walk around the next few months proudly advertising your game by wearing the baseball cap, T-shirt, or sweat shirt they won. Another reason, less obvious but even more important, is that a good in-store demonstration leaves missionaries behind for your product.

Obviously in-store demonstrations are successful only if consumers are available to participate. You must impress on the store managers the importance of promoting the demonstrations in advance. In some cases you may want to offer them co-op advertising for a local newspaper or radio ad. In most cases you should provide "bag stuffers", promotion sheets inserted in each customer's shopping bag for up to thirty days prior to the demonstration. The bag stuffer should titillate, tease, and promise consumers fun and prizes.

Don't make the tournament sound like a serious event. Keep it light. Let them know they can learn to play on the spot, enjoy themselves, and have a chance to win. The bag stuffer is less expensive than co-op advertising, but the co-oping might help you and the store get a story printed about the upcoming event.

Missionary Managers

As a general rule, store managers are busy, over-worked, and under-paid. If you tell them you would like to sit down with them and teach them to play your game so they can better explain it and sell more to customers they are likely to look at you as though you were absolutely out of your mind. If you persist, you are likely to have more of a negative impact than a positive one. On the other hand, a good demo may accomplish exactly what you want.

When you conduct an in-store demonstration or tournament you want to insure people have fun—make that **FUN**—with your game. You want them laughing and joking, raising a good natured ruckus. If they have fun you will sell games. This causes a small miracle. The manager who did not want to take the time to listen to you explain rules learns a lot more about your game as you explain it over and over to different people at the demo. The manager also knows it is a good game because people are having fun and laughing. He knows people like it because they are filling his cash register with money.

When a customer walks in the next week, after you are long gone, and says, "I'm looking for a game for a gift," the manager is likely to say, "You should have been here Saturday. We had a great tournament for this new game. Let me tell you about it." And there you have it—one of the most powerful selling tools available; a retail manager or salesperson who is your missionary. This is terribly important, as you will learn in a moment, because you need re-orders from these independent stores. Establishing a missionary is the best way to ensure you get them.

After the conventions, your next target should be the retail outlets.

INDEPENDENT STORES

Most of the stores you will deal with initially will be of the Mom & Pop variety—small, owner-operated stores, not chain outlets and not franchises. These are the tier one retailers discussed earlier. There are thousands of these in the country, and you can obtain mailing lists for them, broken down by type: toy, gift, game, hobby, etc. An essential facet of your marketing strategy should be to budget mailing advertising flyers to as many of these outlets as you can afford. However, the only way to achieve the level of orders you will need is to stop in and see them. Show them your game. Talk to them and sell them right on the spot and/or conduct a telemarketing campaign.

A strange and interesting fact is that many young game companies go out of business because they have to sell their one product line to these stores. Why do they go out of business? Because initial sales to these independent stores usually are not profitable. In fact, they usually create negative cash flow. How is that possible?

The First Sale: Profitable?

Any professional salesperson who has worked his craft for many years will tell you the first sale to a new customer is the hardest, takes the longest, and is small. It doesn't matter if you are selling real estate on Maui, computers in Chicago, or grits in Georgia, the statistics for making a first sale to a new customer apply. The average first sale occurs after the fifth contact. Let's break this down and see how it impacts profitability.

The customer, in this case an independent toy store, receives your mailing inviting him or her to visit your booth at toy fair (contact number one). The potential customer sees your ad in a trade magazine at toy fair (contact two) and stops by your booth (contact three). After the show you send a follow-up letter thanking him for his time, and enclosing more product/sales information (contact four). When no order arrives you telephone to tell him about your promotion and advertising program but he declines to order "just now" (contact five).

You or your rep stop in to visit and update him on your progress. He orders. Hallelujah! But wait, don't pop the cork yet. He ordered just six games. He really only wanted three, but took six. When you figure in the cost of the games and the proportionate cost of each sales contact, it is easy to see how you have lost money on this sale. The trick is to make sure these retailers reorder. As previously stated, generating reorders is the function of promotions and advertising not sales. It goes without saying reorders also are the function of the game's quality and playability and the word of mouth advertising those features generate.

Love Those Missionaries!

Did I just hear a light switch on? Suddenly the importance of creating missionary managers becomes obvious. They are a major key to generating early and frequent reorders. You have to treat these people like royalty. In the early going they can do more to help you—or hurt you—than anyone else.

A few years ago I helped a lady from Texas produce a game. She was extremely intelligent, but had no knowledge of the game industry. I was apprehensive about her chances for success, but we made the game and delivered it—boxed and ready to ship.

"Boogie on In"

The lady went into action promptly. Her marketing strategy was basic but it turned out to be pretty irresistible. *She was her marketing plan.* She jumped in body and soul, traveling to conventions, fairs, trade shows, art shows—any place she might sell some games. Wherever there was any kind of gathering with a few hundred or a few thousand people in attendance, she was there. On the way to these events she stopped in every town she passed and checked the yellow pages for the names and addresses of local game and toy, book and gift shops. Then, as she put it, she "boogied on in", taking a few copies of her game with her.

As she traveled she sold her games daily, through sheer personal force. This one-woman tornado spent two years sweeping through Texas and Louisiana and the rest of the southwest before heading up to Colorado and California. Her initial sales just about covered the cost of her trips, but she gained more and more exposure for her game with each new stop. Before too long reorders began to come in and it became obvious her game was actually selling. The game is not a blockbuster, but it looks as though it is going to be around for quite a while and give her a nice return on her investment.

As far as I know, other than her travel and direct sales expenses, this enterprising lady has spent less than $5,000 on all the advertising connected with her game. You might not have the time to travel to this extent but the point is this: this lady, selling her inventory to pay for her trips, managed to carve out a niche in the marketplace with only a little additional expense. One reason this method worked? She

created continuous, escalating exposure for the game. The more people hear about a product, the greater the potential there is for increasing sales.

PART 7: Getting Exposure

Basically there are three ways to gain exposure. You can buy it, you can work for it, or you can have it thrust upon you.

BUYING EXPOSURE

Buying exposure means advertising. In the beginning this will be only the second most effective method, but by far the most costly. Buying advertising space in consumer and trade magazines is expensive, but there are other things you can do.

Offering an extra discount to your retailers is one of them. Give them an additional five percent if they will make a window or aisle display of your game and send you a photograph as proof. This works well because window displays are the equivalent of prime time television in retailing. Once a retailer has taken the trouble to set up the display, you can bet it will stay a while.

Another method is to establish an arrangement with one or more mail order houses and conduct what is known as a "per inquiry" or P.I. sales program. The mail order company places an advertisement for the game in its catalog, which they mail to customers. As the orders come in, half the money along with names and addresses of the customers are forwarded to you, and you ship the game. Sometimes it's difficult to convince mail order companies they will get enough business from an item to make running the ad worth their time and money. If you can persuade them, this is a great way to create awareness of the product and generate some sales.

WORKING FOR EXPOSURE

The second way to gain exposure, working for it, is the most common and something you can do on a day-by-day basis. It involves travel, an activity for which there is absolutely no substitute. However, there is an alternative. Make a habit of typing a press release at the end of every month. I know this sounds as though it may be a waste of time, but if your "news" is appropriate and timely it just may get published.

**Press Releases =
Free Advertising**

Let's say you are going to be traveling to a convention in Eureka, Arkansas. Send press releases to as many local and neighboring newspapers as possible, announcing you are coming to demonstrate an exciting new game about (insert a brief description) at the convention, and give the date and location. Mention how long the game has been on the market and how well it is doing. Conclude by telling everyone they are invited.

The game may not be newsworthy—not yet, anyway—but the convention may be and the newspapers may not have been aware of it. They might run the piece more to announce the convention than to plug your game but what difference does it make. As is often the case the newspaper may decide to write its own story and someone will call you for details. Be happy when this happens. It means the story will be longer and you are likely to get an even better plug.

Another way the written word may come in handy is if the game appeals to a specialized market. Those same magazines in which you advertised may be ripe for an article telling how the game can be used to educate people about a particular issue. For example, suppose a game deals with highway construction and you found a magazine called ROADWORK TODAY. Write an article describing how your game teaches people the basic laws and regulations that apply to building highways. If the game is fairly sophisticated, you might even market it as a model for planners and engineers.

These articles must be more than thinly disguised advertisements, however. They must be newsworthy or, at the very least, something fun to read that a publication might be willing to use as filler. Make sure to send copies of every press release to area radio and television stations in addition to the print media. A number of successful games, including *Trivial Pursuit*, were helped because the enterprising game inventors actually had disc jockeys—at no cost—playing them on the air.

Always try to include a local tie-in when you submit articles to local or regional media. If you are promoting to or working with a local social organization your article may offer more appeal.

**College Newspapers—
a Prime Target**

If the game is appropriate, send some releases to college and university newspapers. These publications generally are more receptive and often seek offbeat articles. Most people do not realize *Trivial Pursuit*, *PICTIONARY*, *Pente*, *UNO*, and *DUNGEONS & DRAGONS* were all campus crazes before they hit the big time. College campuses, especially those heavily populated with dormitories, are a closed environment in many respects. Word-of-mouth advertising spreads much more quickly than it does out in the real world. College age people tend to be very enthusiastic about whatever they are into at the moment. If a game becomes the rage on campus there's a good chance the news will spread back home during the holidays.

Retailers with the potential to carry your game are another group to keep in mind. They should receive a copy of each press release and photocopies of each published article. This is a good way to keep the name of a game in front of them. After a little time has passed, they won't remember if they read the article in a magazine or a press release. Even if many of the releases/stories do not get printed, they still have a cumulative effect with buyers.

HAVING EXPOSURE THRUST ON YOU

The third form of publicity—the one most sought after and the kind that is thrust upon you—can be obtained *only* if and when a game gets really hot. When you get this kind of exposure, you are home free.

Every now and then the media "discovers" a new game that is sweeping the nation. Everyone, from the *Wall Street Journal* to the *Congressional Record*, carries stories about it. By the time this occurs the game is apt to be several years old. Having been bought out by a major game producer, the inventor has retired to some South Sea island. If you and your game ever do become darlings of the media, you are in for a wild time. Sales can increase ten or twenty-fold, virtually overnight.

Unfortunately, the only way I know to obtain this kind of attention is to have pre-existing sales of 100,000 copies, with your game already being played by millions. Or you can buy it . . . temporarily. This actually is what we did some years ago.

Do you recall the summer of 1983 when the biggest question in the news was, "Who Shot J.R. Ewing?". We obtained the rights to do a game based on the television show, "Dallas." It cost us a bundle of front money, but we also bought instant recognition. We threw a press party in Dallas that generated more media exposure than we otherwise ever could have afforded. However, as the season dragged on and the mystery was solved, interest waned . . . and so did the coverage. This is why I call it buying *temporary* exposure.

PRESS RELEASES

There are two kinds of game-related press releases. One is brief and to the point and serves as a space filler in magazines and newspapers. The purpose? To keep a company's name and/or its products in front of potential customers. There also are press releases that are news stories, written as full-length articles. For clarification, we'll refer to the first type as a "press release" and the second type as a "story." Together they create public relations, or PR.

As far as media people are concerned, press releases descend on them like swarms of mosquitoes. In order to be noticed, a release has to stand out visually from all the others that arrive in the same batch of mail. A good idea might be to select a simple piece of graphics from the game itself, combine it with the logotype of the product, and have it imprinted on quality stationery. Choose attractive stock, with typeset letterhead and a matching envelope. Make sure to include the words "Press Release" or "For Immediate Release" in large type at the top the sheet. Print several thousand copies of these blank press release letterheads. Then, as press releases are created, take them to a quick copy printer to have the copy printed. If your copier makes clear copies—sharp type and no smudges—reproduce the completed releases on it.

Stories are written and submitted just as if a freelance writer were trying to get them published. Include a note on a press release form as a cover letter and hope the story is good enough to grab the attention of a staff writer. If you have been able to capture their attention, most of the media—print or broadcast—will want to write their own story. What you submit must be newsworthy. It should have some human interest appeal, some local flavor, or be about some current hot topic. Here are a few sample headlines, and what the story might be about:

HOMETOWN POSTMAN MAKES GAME

Story to be sent to local newspapers. Tells of retired postal employee turned game inventor. Why he invented the game, what it's about, etc. Concentrate on human interest element.

SMALLVILLE HOUSEWIVES BECOME GAME TYCOONS

To be sent to magazines written and published primarily for women. Tells of housewives entering the game market. Why they invented this particular game, what they did before, what the game's market is. Include humor and other elements with which other women will identify.

COCAINE GAME TEACHES LESSON

Tells about former cocaine addicts inventing game while in prison.

This last example may be dramatic but stories need a little drama and excitement if they are to be noticed. Always consider the type of publication you are contacting and slant your story accordingly. Once you begin submitting releases and stories outside your local metropolitan area you must look for a connection to interest the media in those areas. Try to tie in your promotions with social and civic groups and local stores. Some sample headlines might look like this.

BAY AREA SINGLES CLUB LOVES PLAYING GAMES

GOLD COAST SENIORS SERIOUS ABOUT FUN

LIONS CLUB ROARS WITH LAUGHTER

PI KAPS CHALLENGE SORORITIES — "LET THE GAMES BEGIN"

Who Should Get Releases? Keep the following in mind.

Radio Stations. Nationwide, but especially local talk shows and stations with a possible interest in interviewing a local inventor. Aim for talk stations as opposed to top forty stations. Send a sample sheet, if possible, describing how the game can be played on the air.

Television Stations. Nationwide again, even though there seems little hope that someone on the Tonight Show's guest booking staff will select you and your game for an appearance. But you never know, and it costs very little to try. Early morning talk shows often need offbeat items and interesting people. Games get more attention from all media around Christmas time but this is doubly true for television.

Local Publications. Newspapers and city magazines (i.e., Philadelphia, Atlanta, Chicago, Dallas, Houston). Slant stories for local flavor, perhaps comparing cities according to numbers of game inventors, markets for games, etc. Tie in your local connections with stores and promotions.

Regional Publications. Those covering a certain geographical area (e.g., *Texas Monthly, Ultra, Southwest Magazine, The New Englander,* and *Florida Today*). Slant stories in much the same way as for city magazines but with more regional flavor.

National Publications. This is the big league (e.g., *Time, Newsweek, U.S. News & World Report, Redbook, Cosmopolitan, Vogue, USA*

Today, and *The Wall Street Journal*). These publications usually carry stories on an item that has remained hot for a prolonged period of time.

Special Interest Magazines. There are magazines for fishermen, hunters, painters, poets, seamstresses, truck drivers, baseball card collectors ... just about any group you could imagine. Many of them are small and welcome well-written articles related to their fields. If you can establish a connection between your game and their readership you will have a good chance of placing a story.

Trade/Industry Magazines. Periodicals that cover specific industries, hobbies, or events related to the subject of the game.

Prospective Buyers. A thorough list should be created and maintained of every potential buyer. Each should receive a copy of every press release or story as it is submitted or published.

PRESS AGENTS & PUBLIC RELATIONS FIRMS

A good press agent or public relations consultant can generate more publicity than normally could be purchased for ten times his fee. Just make sure you fully understand the rate schedule and all the conditions.

Agents and PR people seem to come in two flavors; that is, they seem to specialize in either print or electronic media. The very large agencies certainly have the ability to cover both but they usually charge more than smaller ones. The latter (some are individuals operating from their homes) tend to be less expensive but may be limited in terms of experience, ability, and/or contacts. For example, a particular agent may be familiar with regional newspapers and magazines but have virtually no worthwhile contacts in radio or television.

Because of the costs involved, it's best in the beginning to stick with someone whose primary effectiveness is in print media. If you have the funds to cover both print and electronic media, be sure to hire someone with the ability to set up and book an interview tour. A television tour consists of sending a game inventor around the country, scheduling appearances on local talk shows. With radio talk shows most "tours" can be done over the telephone from the inventor's home or office phone. (These interviews are called "phoners".) Since you will be traveling to conventions anyway, there's a chance your TV appearances can be coordinated with your convention trips.

Pezzano + Company is the Manhattan-based public relations firm which launched both *Trivial Pursuit* and *PICTIONARY* without advertising support. Judith Sussman, the company's executive vice president, is a twenty year industry veteran who speaks annually at the Game Inventors of America's Conference. Judith offers the following "10 Don'ts of P.R."

1. Don't confuse public relations with advertising. Advertisers pay to have their message appear exactly how they want it, where they want it, and when they want it. In public relations you work to convince the reporter to cover your game as news (in a game review, gift round-up, inventor profile, etc.). Public relations therefore is not predictable, but it has far more credibility because the public knows that editorial coverage cannot be bought or guaranteed.

2. Don't approach a reporter without doing your homework. Read your local papers and watch local TV to learn which reporters/shows might cover your game in their lifestyles segments. Also go to your local bookstore or library to get a copy of one or more comprehensive books which deal with public relations.

3. Don't tell reporters (or yourself) that you have the next *Trivial Pursuit* just because your family and friends love playing the game. Do yourself a favor and test the game on active game players you don't know (if possible don't even let them know you are the inventor). The feedback you get back will be more helpful, and may even give you some ideas on how to promote the game.

4. Don't shoot for consumer media coverage "until the ducks are flying." Consumers have very short memories. Don't get coverage until your game is on store shelves. All you will accomplish is getting people into stores looking for your game and buying someone else's.

5. Don't try for national media coverage if you have local distribution. An extension of "Don't #4"—make an overall marketing plan and stick to it! If you start locally with sales, start locally with PR. You only get one shot. (Use your local PR to help sell regionally, use your regional PR to help sell nationally . . . and build the momentum as you grow.)

6. Don't forget the retailers. You have two main target audiences and there are separate media for each. Contact the Toy Manufacturers of America in New York or come to the G.I.A. (Game Inventors of America) Conference to get a list of toy industry trade magazines. Send the editor at each a sample of your game with background information and a black and white photograph.

7. Don't forget specialty media. Go back to the library and look in Bacon's *Publicity Checker* or *Larimi's* for the addresses of specific magazines and those that deal with special-interest themes. For example, if your game has to do with soap operas, readers of *Soap Opera Digest* most likely would be interested in your game. If yours is a geography game, teachers' publications or travel magazines may be interested.

8. Don't forget sampling. Remember that your PR objectives are spreading the word (increasing awareness that your game exists) and personal endorsements (recommendations from media and other influential individuals and groups—from neighbors to community leaders). Seek creative ways to let people sample your game (in-store demonstrations, game nights at the local community center, etc.).

9. Don't think there is a magic formula. Emphasize what is unique and entertaining about your game. Experiment with different approaches and combinations to see what works for your game, within your marketing and budget objectives.

10. Don't give up. . .and DO have fun.

PRODUCT TIE-INS

One thing leads to another. A client of mine was reading a trade magazine looking for new outlets for her game when she came across an article about an upcoming anti-illiteracy campaign sponsored by some heavyweight organizations. Since her product was a word game that fostered literacy (though somewhat indirectly) she saw a tie-in. She sent the game, with a letter, to the campaign headquarters. After several phone calls and meetings, her game was officially sanctioned by the campaign and its sponsors.

This generated immediate sales activity, as associate member organizations learned of the product through conferences and newsletters. The game was made more credible because of its official connection with a noble cause, so my client went off hunting elephants. She convinced a nationwide fast food chain to try a version of her game on its paper placemats, with a blurb supporting the anti-illiteracy campaign. The test went extremely well; the fast food chain commissioned a variety of placemats using the game and paid the inventor a royalty.

This imaginative lady managed to put herself in the position of being paid to promote her product. Tie-ins often involve licenses but this case is a perfect example of one that made rather than cost money.

PART 8: Selling Game Markets

Once your promotions and advertising are in place and working, the third part of the marketing mix takes over. We have discussed previously the traditional game market's three major tiers — the various types of stores that buy and sell games. You may also find some non-traditional markets for your game. Let's take a look at selling each type of store or market.

TRADITIONAL TOY & GAME MARKET

This includes retail stores and wholesalers who generally carry popular games on a year-round basis. This group normally is the largest potential market for games. It is comprised of every type of store or distributor with games on their shelves year-round, ranging from the Mom & Pop stores to mass merchandisers like K-Mart, Toys-R-Us, and Sears.

Mass Merchandisers

The mass merchandisers have the ability to put your game in the big leagues. Unfortunately they tend to be interested only in games that are proven winners; games offered by major manufacturers with a lot of money to spend on advertising. If you are able to break into this market, you will have the advantage of selling high volume to solid companies certain to pay for the goods. The disadvantages you'll find are that you will have to work like the devil to get into this market and then you will virtually have to give your product away.

You will end up being a banker of sorts, shipping games as early as April and May but not receiving any payment until October. The real kicker here is that if your game takes off, you will receive several large reorders that will have to be financed before the giant chains will even think about paying you for the first shipment.

The buyers for these chains are bombarded daily by every toy and game entrepreneur in existence. You will have to present substantial evidence to convince these folks to take a gamble on your product. It won't be all that difficult to get an appointment with them, but you are likely to find yourself up against a polite stone wall unless your game and/or promotion is perceived as being red hot.

EDUCATIONAL MARKET

This market includes retail and wholesale distribution, public and private schools, and libraries that sell or use items intended for education either in a school setting or at home.

While many pre-school and early school games cross over into the type of market described above, there also are many aimed directly at educators and institutions. This market does not offer the potential sales of the traditional market, but it can be a good starting point for a new game. There are wholesalers and retailers serving this market specifically, as well as some fairly big direct mail catalogue operations.

In addition, there is the more obvious route of selling to educators and institutions via telemarketing and state and national shows and conferences. The key to this market will be your ability to demonstrate the tangible educational value of your product, and a method for using it in a classroom setting.

BOOK MARKET

This market includes retail and wholesale operations and public and private libraries that sell or lend various items, but primarily books.

This market is larger than the toy/game market in that more money is spent on books in this country than on toys and games. There are more book retailers because of this, and if a game fits into a major book merchandiser's plans, it may do decent volume with a few major accounts. However, not every game is suitable for this market. The ones that have done well in the past have had some kind of tie-in with popular books. For example, *Trivial Pursuit* did well in the book market long before it became a mass merchandised item, because buyers knew that trivia books had done well for a number of years. Word games always seem to be the most likely entries into this market because of their natural connection with books.

Since the success of *Trivial Pursuit* (and other games like it) in this market, buyers seem a little less resistant to opening small game sections in their stores. They cannot carry the more common popular games so they must consider lesser known items, and that creates an opportunity for quality products with the appropriate subject matter.

GIFT AND STATIONERY MARKET

This market comprises retail and wholesale operations engaged in marketing gift items in general. For all practical purposes this category will be treated the same as the gift market except that there are often separate trade shows for stationery items. In addition, many department store chains sell high-priced adult games in their stationery sections.

According to past marketing surveys, half the games purchased in the United States are bought as gifts. Obviously they are not all bought in "gift stores," but this market should not be overlooked. There are over 60,000 gift shops in the country. If a game establishes itself here, it has a good chance of being around for a while.

Then there are the stationery departments usually found in retail chains. They tend to carry a select few games not normally available through mass merchandisers. While these outlets cannot sell millions of games, they do quite well and they tend to be more open to trying new products. One big disadvantage is that they tend to drop games as the novelty wears off, so be prepared to see a huge slump in sales after the second year of dealing with buyers at these accounts. While it may be easier to enter this market than others, it still isn't a cinch. You must have a first class product. It can stand to be a little pricey, but it must be top quality.

SPECIALTY MARKET

This is a market or industry not normally exposed to games. With the right subject matter, however, it can provide a sales opportunity for a particular game.

Here's where a game can really shine. This is a market uncluttered by other games and one that will accept a higher retail price tag. Sound like a perfect place for your game? Let's see!

A few years ago I was involved in producing a game based on leasing land and drilling for oil. It was a beautiful game with a large number of quality components and excellent play value. It also was expensive to produce and had a suggested retail value of $35, high for the traditional board game market at the time. The inventor decided not to go after traditional markets, but concentrated instead on a few retail outlets and a handful of the most exclusive stores in the country.

His principal target market was the oil and gas industry, where there was no game competition at all. Most of the marketing was directed toward large, prosperous firms who could afford to buy up to a thousand games to give as gifts to clients and prospective customers. Instead of settling for the $14-16 they would get from a distributor, the game's producers pulled in $20-24 a unit on a direct sale basis. After demand was established here, they planned to edge slowly into the mass market.

Another example of a specialty game is currently coming out of the planning stages and getting ready for production. It's a real estate development game which the owners intend to market in a similar manner to the oil game. Virtually all their efforts will go into direct mail and telemarketing aimed at commercial real estate brokers and developers, construction companies, city planners, and architectural firms. In addition, they plan to attend trade shows. This game also carries a suggested retail price of $35 and is being pushed as a one of a kind gift item. A third game currently in development is intended for the medical industry. The expected retail price will be a very substantial $80-90.

One feature all these games have in common is very high quality and a sophisticated look. No corners have been cut to save money, which means the negative side of this approach is production cost. The games are expensive to produce, but in a specialized, non-competitive market they can demand a high price tag. When considering this market, determine how much you can afford to spend to obtain the quality look you need.

THE PSYCHOLOGY OF BUYING

Before plunging into a discussion of the four sub-markets, let's consider what they have in common—and that is the buyers. If the old adage is true—"Nothing happens until somebody sells something"—it follows that there is no sale until somebody buys something. And therein lies the challenge. Buyers are not a stagnant group. They usually are on their way up, down, or out. Only a masochist would want to be a buyer. They are under constant pressure to produce while computers keep an eye on their progress. The more important the store they work for, the more demand is placed on their time by every individual and firm with an item to sell. With computers coldly calculating the results of their decisions, it may be easier to move a mountain than to persuade buyers who have established a successful department to make a change.

When a salesperson pushing a new item sits down with a buyer, he really is asking the buyer to do a lot more than just to try his product. Every department or section of a store is expected to generate a profit, which is usually based on the square footage of the area. For the department to generate its required profit, each item offered for sale must meet certain minimums. If one item falls below expectations, it reduces overall profit and is replaced. Through a process of experience, knowledge, instinct, and nervous sweat each buyer strives to create a department that at the very least meets the minimum.

Enter the unknown: a new salesperson with a new item from a new company. It's enough to terrify any self-respecting buyer who has sweated blood to establish better-than-average profits. Here is this person trying to convince him to replace an item that is at least meeting minimum requirements with a product that has virtually no proven sales record. Furthermore, the new item may or may not be made by a company that will be able to meet higher demands should sales zoom. "No thank you, sir," he says.

Get the picture? Forget about outselling *MONOPOLY*; you had better be able to convince the buyer your game will do better than the least successful game he has on his shelf.

Are You an Authorized Vendor?

A second (perhaps minor) objection often raised by store buyers is this. They cannot buy from you until you have been registered by their firm as an authorized vendor. To register a vendor, a retailer expends between $2,000 and $4,000 worth of man hours and computer time. The buyer won't get excited about having all this expense attributed to his department for a single item that might not even sell.

You will hear a lot of objections to one-item lines for this reason, in addition to everything involved in just processing the order. There is no pat answer to this objection but it is heartening to note that *PICTIONARY, Pente, UNO,* and even *Trivial Pursuit* were once one-item lines. This is not an insurmountable problem, but you are going to have to work hard to persuade the buyer your product is worth the extra effort.

The best advice I can offer in dealing with game buyers is to be patient, honest, and sincere. They don't like to turn vendors down, but their job demands it a good deal of the time. It is best not to try to push them into a corner. You have to ask for the order—that's your job—but their job is to say "yes" or "no." If you force a decision, you may just be forcing a "no."

Now on to the prospect of selling to major markets through their sub-markets.

THE SUB-MARKETS

Selling by Direct Mail

Using direct mail has some distinct advantages and disadvantages when compared with other marketing strategies. Its principal advantage is that it brings in the full retail price (there are no discounts involved) in addition to the two or three dollars charged for postage and handling. Let's look at a hypothetical print run of 2,500 games that cost $7.88 each to produce. Assuming we managed to sell them all through direct mail at the full retail price of $16, we realized gross sales of $40,000, less COG of $19,700. This means a net profit of $20,300—103% return on the original investment before we deduct our cost of sales.

Realistically, this is not likely to happen, but you get the point. Direct mail sales, no matter the volume, can generate a high profit margin and a positive cash flow; i.e., more money is coming in than going out. The other advantage of direct mail sales is its effect on word-of-mouth advertising. People who buy games through the mail tend to play those games and tell others about them.

The down side to this method is the cost of advertising. Ads have to appear constantly in magazines where potential customers are likely to see them. I have been told an ad needs to appear three times in consecutive issues to be effective. And you are apt to be more successful if all three ads are different, as people tend to pass over advertisements they already have read. In addition, you should realize that ads do not necessarily pay for themselves right away. People tend to put magazines aside for a while, picking them up again at a later date. What this means is that you will be paying for the ads over a period of time. There are price breaks at different frequency levels (3X, 6X, etc.) but the ads had better pull enough sales to cover their cost.

Another disadvantage to direct sales is the processing of orders. When you are selling one game at a time, orders have to be filled one game at a time. Each item must be packaged, addressed, recorded, and then shipped. If mail order sales are strong and steady, consider hiring a young person to work after school. Better yet, draft one of your own children. (It probably is about time they started to earn their keep anyway.) In any event, regardless of how happy you are to get them, processing those one game orders can become a tedious task.

Be sure to get corrugated wrappers to protect your games in shipment. These usually can be obtained from companies who maintain stocks of standard size boxes, or you can have them custom made. If your mail order business volume is not great, you probably are better off buying a few at a time from someone who stocks them, even though they may not be an exact fit. If a hundred or more games a week are being shipped on a direct mail basis, it may be wise to have some made to your specifications. If you do that, don't have cartons made. Wrappers are cheaper and do just as well. Tell the box maker you want the kind of wrapper used to ship books. He will know what you are talking about.

Catalog Sales

An alternative to doing your own direct mail sales is to sell your game to various catalog companies for inclusion in their catalogs. Granted you are back to selling at a 50% discount but you save the cost of advertising. There are dozens of major mail order catalog houses in the U.S. and hundreds of smaller ones who offer games. The easiest way to begin researching them is to visit your library and study a copy of *The Direct Mail Market Place.*

Before moving on to another market, let's reexamine some of the ways direct mail sales can be obtained. The most common way is magazine advertising. This can be extremely costly if the ad is not effective. Do some research on both the magazines and the other direct mail ads which appear regularly in them. Find out about the readers. In some cases it may be necessary to design a special ad for a magazine. When using this approach make sure to "key" the ads; i.e., add a code to the address that will tell you the orders came from a specific ad in a specific magazine.

Keep records of the results. They will show you where your advertising investment is working and where it is not. After 60-90 days of running ads and evaluating results, you may decide to run a larger ad in a magazine which pulled well, and/or drop an ad from one that did not. Continuing to run an advertisement in a magazine which is not pulling in orders is just wasting money. Pay attention to this area. You soon will learn how to get the most out of your mail order advertising investment.

Direct Mail/Direct Sales

The next market area is retail outlets, almost all independents (non-chain), and mostly the mom and pop operations. There are thousands of these stores and they should become an excellent source of sales. They actually are easier to reach than consumers but more difficult to sell. They offer a different set of advantages and disadvantages.

BUYING A MAILING LIST

The least expensive way to reach these retailers is go to the yellow pages and find a company that supplies mailing lists. Call and ask them if they have a list of "X" number of a certain type of store. They will check, call back, and tell you what is available and how much it is going to cost. Then you have a mailing piece printed and give it to the mailing house to send to your newly-acquired list.

This is the least expensive method I know to reach large numbers of prospective buyers in a highly concentrated market. When buying the list, ask if it is possible to obtain a computer printout of the names and addresses with phone numbers. If a list with phone numbers is not available, try to get a list without numbers and go to the library to look them up. You want to do this so you can move into then next phase—telemarketing.

Back to your mailing program for a moment. It really won't hurt to mail your piece "Bulk Rate." It is the lowest postage cost. Each item mailed takes a little longer to get where it's going, but it does get there. What is really important, however—whether it's mailed bulk rate, first class, registered, or certified—is the piece itself. It has to be eye catching, interesting, appealing, unusual, and to the point. If it isn't, it will find its way to the circular file within ten seconds after it has been opened.

The flyer *has* to make an impression. You hope it will inspire at least a few mail or phone orders. But even if it does not, it still needs to have an impact so these merchants will remember the product when they are called or mailed to again.

When you design the flyer, feel free to "borrow" from the magazine ads you have seen and liked. On this first mailing piece especially, a good picture of the game is essential, and it must be large enough to be easily identifiable. Another essential ingredient is large, bold type announcing the discount available to retailers.

Many stores buy staple, non-game, and toy items through distributors whenever they can. In this case, there will not be any distributors at the onset, so make the retailers aware (in both the flyer and in follow-up phone calls) that the item is not available through normal distribution channels. At this point you are selling direct to stores.

When a retailer buys from a distributor his discount usually is 40% off the retail price. If an item has a suggested retail price of $10.00, the retailer pays the distributor $6.00 and he receives the goods freight paid. When a retailer buys direct from the factory, will expect a 50% discount because now he pays the freight costs.

THE PROMPT PAYMENT DISCOUNT

One thing which works well is to offer an additional discount for prompt payment. Normal terms in both the toy and gift markets state that invoices are payable 30 days after receipt of goods. To help create positive cash flow and keep both accountants and creditors happy, try offering these terms on larger orders: 50% net 30; 10% net ten days. What all this means is the dealer earns the 50% discount if he pays the invoice within 30 days of receiving the merchandise and an additional 10% if he pays within ten days. That is not 10% off the top. If you are not familiar with discount structures, now is the time to become so. Here is an example that should help.

A game retails for $30.00. A store buys 72 copies, for a total retail value of $2,160. The store's discount is 50%, net 30 days, which means it owes $1,080 if payment is made within 30 days. If the retailer is managing his business effectively (and enjoying a positive cash flow), he will pay within ten days to get the extra 10% discount. Then he only pays $972. This is how it works:

Retail value equals	$2,160.00
50% discount	1,080.00
Net due in 30 days	1,080.00
10% prompt payment discount	-108.00
Net due in ten days	$972.00

It really is simple. Whenever a string of discounts appear, the first applies to the retail value; any others apply in sequence against the preceding net amount. In this case the 50/10% discounts add up to an aggregate 55% off retail.

Mom & Pop Stores: Good Business?

Mom and Pop type operations can be very good business for game sales ... sometimes. By and large the owners and operators of these stores are hard working folks who pay attention to their local market and know almost instinctively what will and what won't sell in their stores. No matter how positive they "feel" about a new product, especially one not offered by a major manufacturer with strong advertising support, they are likely to be skeptical and cautious at first. They probably will want to order six or less of the item to see how it does. Some may even try to buy on consignment. Initially these small quantities—even the consignment orders—will be all right, assuming the buyers are paying the shipping charges, because of a point of view which typically exists in these small stores.

If three copies of a game go to a store and are all sold within two weeks, the retailer notices, to his pleasant surprise, that he is sold out. It creates a re-ordering frame of mind. But if six copies are sold to the same store and if three of them are left at the end of the same two week period, the frame of mind created is negative. The merchant thinks he bought too many and the item is not moving well. The moral, of course, is don't oversell these people. It's far better, in the long run, to let them order small quantities at first. If the game starts to do well, and they continue to run out and reorder, they will have nothing but praise for the product. That attitude will become a significant factor in further increasing sales. It may not seem important, but in an independent retail operation, the owner's and employees' attitude about a product is everything. These are not huge, impersonal discount houses. These are small shops with a lot of repeat customers. The people who work there can only compete with the mass merchandisers by offering service. The service they offer is, more often than not, courtesy and knowledge of the products on their shelves. When a customer asks, "What's a good game to buy?", you want them to say, "This one is really doing well. Why not try it?"

So, a modest sales approach is right for this market. Even if you have a friend who owns a store, resist the urge to take advantage of that relationship by selling him three hundred copies of the game at one time. It won't help either of you.

Telemarketing   Overcoming the skepticism and caution of these buyers is going to require determination. It will be necessary to contact them repeatedly by mail or phone, as well as in person whenever possible. Send the same piece two or three times. Send post cards. In fact a post card can be an effective and inexpensive method of mailing follow-ups.

One lady I know had a full color picture of her game printed on card stock and cut into postcards. She mailed a normal eight and one-half by eleven inch advertisement initially then began making her follow-up calls. As she made each call, she kept a customer card for each shop, filling it in with as much information as she could gather, including the names of the owners and, more importantly, the person who ordered games, and just about anything else that was passed on in conversation. These people, once they open up, love to talk about their stores and their knowledge of the industry, but getting them to open up is difficult. The lady would try to chat with each store she called, introducing herself and her product as a first effort. She made no bones about letting them know she wanted them to buy her game, but she didn't push it too hard. When they started to make some excuse to get off the phone she would change the subject by asking what games sold best in their store, or what kind of people frequented their shop—anything to keep the person talking. As the merchant spoke, she made notes on a sheet of scratch paper while watching a clock. When the timer was approaching three minutes she would politely bring the conversation to a close by telling the person several things. She told them she had to get off the phone before the long distance charges bankrupted her. She genuinely appreciated their time and would like to call them again to ask their opinion (people love to give opinions) about the best way to go about marketing her item. Then she asked if it would be all right if she called them back on a certain day about a month away. When they agreed to a date, she thanked them again for their time and said something like, "Well, it's really been pleasant speaking with you. You have been very helpful. You must really know this business. I'm looking forward to talking to you again, when I can afford it. When I call we'll write an order, OK?"

Now this may seem very innocent, but believe me it's not. In fact this woman was a deadly phone salesperson. The number of orders she took on her second or third call was phenomenal. The reason for this success—her manner and tactics.

Her first call was very casual, not pushy, though she told them quickly she called to sell games. After that she let it rest, drawing them out with questions about subjects they could speak on knowledgeably. The more the other person spoke, the more confident they became and the less intimidated they were by talking to a "salesperson". When she closed the conversation she made them aware she was not rich. Most of them aren't either and identified with that. Then she made an appointment to call again, creating a certain feeling of obligation on the part of the person to whom she was speaking. At the very end she announces that she will ask for an order from them and asked if this would be "OK". This sets the person up to give her an order on the next call. Even if the person is not consciously aware he or she is committing to place an order when they next speak, the suggestion has been planted.

After the call is over, the lady fills out her customer card with the information she has obtained. Then, before calling the next number, she writes out a post card saying something relevant and personal, confirming the date of her next call. The card is then put into a date folder and mailed two weeks from the day.

No one can guarantee the results of any system, but of all the results I've seen from people entering the game market for the first time, this approach is one of the most effective. True, it requires time and money; but about the third time you call these people you could be closing (getting orders) as many as fifteen percent. As these shops become your customers, calls become more productive. You can stop mailing every month and concentrate on opening new markets. But before going on to some of those new markets, let's look at some basic rules for making telephone sales.

Ask for an Order!   The golden rule is ASK FOR AN ORDER! No matter how indirect or easy your manner, not asking is wasting time and money. When I train someone to work the phones I make it a point to get them to ask for the order at least three times during the conversation. I want them to be polite, and not overly pushy, but if they don't ask, it's not very likely they will make a sale. Some ways of asking politely could be, "could I get you to try...", "Could you test my product by taking...", or, in a half joking manner, "What do I have to do to get you to give this a try?" You'll come up with your own style to suit your personality. But remember, if you're not going to ask, don't bother to call.

The second rule of telemarketing is Stay on the Phone. You are playing a numbers game. If you don't believe playing the odds really works, check out the insurance industry. Their whole business is based on statistics. They have, are, and always will make fortunes. There is an interesting story I once heard about a real estate agent who was using telemarketing to sell land in Hawaii. It's worth repeating because it clicks perfectly with all types of telephone sales.

This industrious, determined fellow created a list of around fifty thousand island residents who were likely prospects. He set up a telephone marketing room, hired and trained people to man the phones, and then dove right in. Each month, every person on the list was contacted regarding a specific real estate investment offer.

After a few months, many of the people were getting down-right rude, telling the callers never to bother them again. Undaunted, the callers kept calling ... every month. At first it seemed the operation was destined to fail. There were some sales, but they fell far short of expectations. Then things began to turn around. About a year into the operation an analysis of the records revealed some interesting things.

Persistence Pays   Some of the people who had been rude and insisted on not being called again had invested. After the first investments, people tended to become more or less regular clients. But the most amazing statistic retrieved was the fact that eighty percent of the people investing for the first time did so after the fifth contact.

Interestingly enough, our own telemarketing program selling games to retail outlets produced almost identical results. In addition, several other telemarketing studies offer similar statistics to back up the findings. The lesson is fairly obvious; persistence pays off.

On days when you are working at telemarketing, try to make at least fifty contacts a day. As soon as each call is finished make an accurate record of what was said. This record keeping can be best done using a computer data base or a card system, which can be accessed by date. This allows you to see easily when people are to be called back.

Telemarketing is just like any other form of sales. If insults, rudeness, and people saying, "No", cause a loss of faith in yourself or product, you're better off dropping the project before it costs a fortune; or at least make arrangements to have someone else do the selling.

Everyone is a little nervous when calling someone they don't know. It's natural, but try to put things in perspective. You're not making first contact with an alien race, you are calling another human, one probably just as nervous as you are. When working on the phone, try to stay as relaxed as possible. Smile, even though nobody can see—it sets a frame of mind and mood. Talk as though you already know the person; after all, if it's a call back—you do.

Telemarketing is a great way to tie your whole marketing program together. Here is a sample of how the people who promoted *U.S.A. Trivia* made their plan work.

The telemarketer calls a local game store and conveys the following information. *U.S.A. Trivia* is a great new game being promoted in your area. The inventor, known as Mr. Trivia, is going to be on radio station WBLA in your city in four weeks. He and the host play the game with call-ins. If anyone can beat him he gives them a coupon good for one free game at a local store that carries the item. We would like for you to be that store this session. In addition, Mr. Trivia will come to your store the evening after the radio show and conduct an in-store demonstration. If you will participate in this promotion he will plug your store and the demonstration on the radio. We will provide you with two hundred bag stuffers to promote the event to your customers. If you will run a local newspaper or radio ad we will co-op up to fifty percent of the cost in merchandise at retail value.

Wow! If you present this in a logical, friendly, not too pushy manner, as if you are giving the store an opportunity to participate in a new program: if you make it absolutely clear the store has nothing to lose you can see how effective it can be.

There are many good telemarketing books available. They contain a tremendous amount of information. If telemarketing is part of the plan, get them and use them.

Two more things. The first is to follow up the call with a mailing. Whether it's simply a post card confirming your next appointment or a brochure or copies of some press coverage of the game, it's very important to reinforce the personal relationship established with the call.

The last rule of telemarketing is the first rule; ask for the order. It doesn't matter how indirectly, but work it in to the conversation at least three times. You will be amazed at how many people will relent the third time and try your product.

Distributors and Chain Stores

The next sales areas to think about are game distributors and chain stores. Though they share some similarities, the buying habits of both differ from those of single retail outlets.

The few distributors remaining in the toy industry tend to buy larger quantities, but demand better discounts. A distributor may not buy at all unless the terms are at least 50/10 with freight paid and invoice coming due on the tenth of the month, thirty days after receipt of goods. Remember, that's fifty percent off the retail, then ten percent off the remaining fifty percent. In this case the ten percent is not for prompt payment: it may be necessary to throw in another five or ten percent to cover this area.

If a distributor has any faith at all in an item he usually will order a gross (twelve dozen). However, they tend to be cautious when ordering new, unknown items and may start with as few as twenty-four or thirty-six. A distributor who deals with volume may not order at all until he becomes convinced he'll be able to move at least a gross; otherwise it just isn't worth the paperwork involved in adding a new item to inventory.

Chain stores tend to order quantities based on placing so many of an item in each store. This can vary from as few as six to as many as a gross, depending upon the chain's traffic pattern and volume history. In this case it may be necessary to "drop-ship"; i.e., split the order and ship to various locations. Some chains rely on distributors when trying something new. Others will take six for each of a few stores to test market the item. In any event, if a large chain picks up a new item and does well with it, it can become very lucrative even though each store isn't taking a lot individually. For instance, if a chain with three hundred stores is taking six copies of a game for each store every month a quick calculation shows 1,800 games per month. That's a whopping 20,600 games a year—from one customer!

But before you start opening the champagne, bear firmly in mind the fact that it's not all that easy to get these people to even try a new product. Most keep a close watch on the market. If a game is selling they know about it by keeping a "manager's want list". Since most chains are fairly strict about what goes in their stores they don't allow individual managers much leeway to add something which is not being ordered by their central purchasing department. They do, however, ask each manager to keep a list of items customers are asking for but are not stocked. If a particular item appears several times on numerous manager's lists, the central buyers begin investigating.

Discounts for chain stores may have very similar bottom lines to those for distributors—but getting to the bottom line is often by a different route. For example, the discount will probably start at fifty/ten percent off retail. Another five to ten percent may be included as an advertising allowance for the chain, and an additional five may be given for special placement of the game (i.e., an end of the aisle—called an end cap— or window display). Finally, most will ask for two percent if payment is made within thirty days of the due date. So what you might wind up with is a discount which looks something like this: 50/10/5/5/2.

If you are fortunate enough to sell to one of the really large retail chains, don't be surprised to find you suddenly have become a banker as well as a game entrepreneur. In addition to the string of negotiated discounts the chains want something else, something just as important as money—time.

One of the terms with which you'll become familiar in the toy business is "dating". No, you're not about to be taken to dinner and romanced. In the toy industry, as well as in several others, dating terms are applied when a retailer/wholesaler buys a product and has it shipped in the summer, with the first payment due far into the future. For example, in the toy industry, the normal dating payment dates are October 10, December 10 and January 10.

What this means to a small game company is that games will be shipped in April or May to a retailer's units with first payment due on October 10. If the game does well the retailer may reorder in June or July with a new payment date of December 10. Another reorder comes in for September with a January 10 payment date. If it's a big chain and the game's doing well, the game company could have shipped tens of thousands of copies over a seven to eight month period and not have been paid a dime.

As if dating wasn't bad enough, "anticipation" will cause ulcers among the few game companies that stayed around to try and lasso one of these major chains. Anticipation happens when the chain realizes they are buying lots of games from a company and will be reordering according to a previously negotiated dating program. The chain will pay early —that's the good news. The bad news is they will want an additional discount. Let's say the chain took a ten thousand dollar order in March with October 10 dating. For whatever reasons they decide to pay the bill four months early, say June. On the day they cut the check, they'll document the prime annual interest rate, divide by twelve to come up with an equivalent monthly rate then multiply by the number of months early they're paying. The result is a percentage of the bill which gets deducted before the check is mailed to the manufacturer. For example: the chain owes ten thousand dollars which is due on October tenth; the annual interest rate is twelve percent and the chain is paying four months early. Twelve percent divided by twelve months is one percent per month multiplied by four months equals four percent of ten thousand dollars or four hundred dollars which is deducted from the bill.

Unless the distributor or chain store is a very specialized operation it is difficult to get these people to place a first order. Calling them till you're blue in the face may help but in many cases they prefer to see samples, know exactly where the item is being advertised and how often, who else is carrying the item and, "Who's your rep?"

Distributors and chain stores should and can become the biggest market for a game. But at first, until the game has generated genuine demand in the marketplace, concentrate on direct mail, smaller retail outlets and, if there is one, a specialty market.

Appendices

COPYRIGHTS, PATENTS AND TRADEMARKS

Since I am not an attorney and do not carry the necessary insurance to speak freely on the subject of legal protection, (and since I am both lazy and wise enough to let someone else do the work for me if possible) and since this book desperately needs a section on this subject, I have procured the required information from a friend named Tom Timmons. Tom is a founding partner of Timmons & Kelly, a Dallas-based law firm specializing in, among other things, trademarks, patents, and copyrights.

In today's legalistic world it's virtually impossible to stay successful without the services of at least one good lawyer. Picking one to contribute to this work reminded me of my favorite attorney story.

It seems a very wealthy industrialist called his three most trusted associates and friends — his accountant, priest, and attorney — to his death bed. Looking pale and weak, he handed each of them a thick, sealed envelope and said, "I've always disliked the old saying, `you can't take it with you', and I've figured a way to beat it. Each of those envelopes contains 100 thousand dollars in cash. After I have been lowered into the grave and everyone else has left, I want you three to toss those envelopes into the grave then stay until the hole is filled."

The three men looked at each other strangely but tucked the envelopes away and left. A few weeks later, at their friend's funeral they followed his last wishes, throwing the envelopes in and watching the workers fill the hole. As the sun was going down they sat silently in the back seat of a limousine headed toward town.

Halfway there the accountant turns to the priest and says, "Father, I must confess, I couldn't stand watching the money be thrown away. There were only 60 thousand dollars in my envelope."

"Glory Be," says the priest, greatly relieved, "I must confess myself, I couldn't stand the thought of all that money going to waste and I took fifty thousand out for the poor box."

"I am appalled. I am shocked!" said the lawyer, "We were his best friends, his most trusted associates. It was his dying request, for God's sake. I just want the record to show that in my envelope there was my personal check for one hundred thousand dollars."

The point of the story is some lawyers exist solely to make a damn fine living in the legal jungle they have grown around us, others are there to make a fine living as well as to help a few people in the process. Tom is one who has always been there to help when I needed advice.

Protecting Your Game

One of the worst shocks a game inventor can experience is to discover he or she has accidentally dedicated it to the public or unintentionally shared whatever rights exist with a commercial artist. These problems can be avoided and certain protections can be built into the game as it is developed. Ideally, you would like to protect the concept of the game itself, the main idea. You also want to protect the appearance of the game, the artwork which appears on the box, board, rules, cards you would like to protect whatever words are used for the game, including the way the rules are expressed in addition to any writing appearing on the gameboard or playing cards. Finally, in order to eventually have valuable trademark rights, you must use a trademark correctly from the beginning. Probably the simplest guide to obtain these different kinds of protection is simply to purchase a similar type of game which is produced by a major manufacturer. Study the way that manufacturer protects its own game, and that can provide a guide for your own use. We can begin by picking up a *SCRABBLE* crossword game manufactured by Selchow & Righter Co.

Protecting the Concept— Patents and Trade Secrets

There are only two ways of protecting a concept, through patents and trade secrets. As you open the *SCRABBLE* box and lay open the board, notice the notation "Patent No. 2,752,158." It's known as a "patent notice" and it serves to notify people the game is patented (or rather it was patented since that patent expired many years ago). A patent is nearly an ideal form of protection since it does protect the general concept, at least to the extent that the concept meets the requirements of being patentable. In order to be a patentable invention, an item must be new, useful, and unobvious. The general concept of a board game is, of course, not new and neither is the idea of a board game with tiles or cards or dice. It is, however, possible to have a board game made up of those elements which is new in the way it combines those elements.

Patents have several problems, not the least of which is they are expensive and difficult to obtain. Plan on spending a minimum of $4,000 before obtaining a patent on even a fairly simple concept. Also plan on a minimum of months from the time the application is first filed before it issues. Finally, patent applications undergo a tough examination and are frequently rejected.

One final word about patents is worthwhile since there is such widespread misunderstanding concerning them. Patents are not self-enforcing. The government does not enforce a patent except occasionally in the case of infringing imports, so you must be prepared to go to court to enforce your patent. The good news is patents are usually respected; and even in a situation where there is infringement, it normally can be stopped without having to go to court. Infringers have to worry about court costs and attorneys' fees as much as patent owners, but they have the additional worry of possible damage payments to the patent owner.

There is one other way of protecting a concept, through trade secrets. While a game is being developed it can be kept secret. In order to keep it a secret, it is necessary to have confidentiality agreements with everyone who is told about the game. This includes printers, artists and even potential investors. The confidentiality agreements need to describe the game in sufficient detail to identify it, but not in such detail as to give away any secret information in the agreement itself. It can be quite a trick but it can be done.

Artwork and Writings— Copyrights

Look on the inside of the *SCRABBLE* box lid where the rules of play are printed. At the bottom of the rules is the copyright notice, "Copyright 1948, 1949, 1953 by Selchow & Righter Co." The three years listed mean the words used to describe the rules for playing were first published in 1948 and they were then changed sufficiently in 1949 and 1953 to justify registering copyrights for the new editions. The copyright does not protect the general concept, but it does protect the way the rules are expressed. Whereas, a patent only lasts for 17 years from the date it issues, copyrights last for 75 years from the date of first publication for corporate authors and run years past the death of the last joint author for individuals. Now look at the game-board again, on the lower right hand corner there's another copyright notice, "Copyright 1948 by Selchow & Righter Co." This one copyrights the artwork on the game board. If the *SCRABBLE* crossword game had artwork on the box it would also be copyrighted and bear its own copyright notice.

There are two aspects to copyright. One is the copyright notice which includes either the word "Copyright" or "Copr." or the letter "C" written in a circle along with the year the particular copyrighted word, the particular board or set of rules, is first made available to the public and the name of the copyright owner. The copyright notice must appear on every copy of the game. If a game does not show the copyright notice, there is a danger of dedicating your artwork and words to the public.

The second aspect to remember about the copyright is the registration. The registration is a formality but should be done as soon as possible. It is not necessary to obtain the registration or even to file it before publication or printing the notice. Registrations are relatively inexpensive, normally running no more than a couple of hundred dollars even through an attorney.

Protecting Trademarks   Examine the lid of the *SCRABBLE* box. The trademark *SCRABBLE* appears on the top of the box and on all four edges in bold capital letters. In all five places, the description term "crossword game" appears written below the trademark in much smaller letters. In every case, the letter "R" is written in a small circle to the upper right of the trademark. The circled "R" is proper notice the trademark *SCRABBLE* is registered with the U.S. Patent and Trademark Office. You are not permitted to even apply for federal registration unless the game is actually being sold in at least two states or in international commerce. Once the federal registration is applied for it could easily be a year or more before the registration is granted. What you are allowed to use is the combination of the letters "TM" which tells the world "this is my trademark and not a generic term." You do not need a registration in order to use the TM. Even without a registration, the rights obtained strictly from usage can still be valuable and enforceable.

The *SCRABBLE* trademark also appears on the insides of the cover at the beginning of the rules as well as on all four edges of the game board. In total, the trademark appears on the box and board 11 times. In every case, the trademark is in large bold letters. Every time it appears on the outside of the box, it is accompanied by the descriptive term "crossword game" as well as the trademark registration notice. This is good trademark usage and a good model to follow.

Computer games differ from board games in that they also have computer software which can be copyrighted. Once again, it is a good idea to take an established company's product as a model. The *INFOCOM* games are especially creative in the way they call a user's attention to the copyright notice which appears on the screen. In addition, you will find a copyright notice in the written material and on the diskette label. The *INFOCOM* games also illustrate a different example of trademark usage. The trademark *INFOCOM* is the "house mark" for a series of computer games. Each computer game within the series also bears its own trademark such as *SORCERER* or *ENCHANTER*. The use of both trademarks on the same game is not inconsistent since one represents the entire line and the other represents the particular product.

Finally, one special caution needs to be made with regard to copyrights. Pretend for a moment you have just developed an extraordinary computer game, but you need help in writing the computer software. You engage an independent contractor to write the program for you, but have no written agreement or one which makes no mention of copyright ownership. The independent contractor develops the software according to specifications and delivers it. You hand the contractor a check for the agreed amount. The independent contractor thanks you for the check and on his way out mentions, "I hope you like the software which I developed for you. By the way, let me know if you would also like the right to sell it to other people." You know it has not been a good day. The same thing can happen when an independent artist develops the artwork for your game! You need written agreement with all independent contractors, and the written agreements need to specify that the independent contractor will assign all copyrights to you.

It may be possible to file for some of the registrations yourself but I don't recommend it. As I said before, it's a crazy world; a brewery in Colorado can get sued over a drunk driving accident in California because the driver drank their beer. Get a lawyer, you'll sleep better and so will I.

TRADE SHOWS AND CONVENTIONS

The following is a list of trade shows and conventions which may be helpful in bringing a game to market. Each industry usually will have its own trade shows and if a game legitimately bridges two or more industries it may be a good idea to attend shows in all of those industries. On the other hand, if the game really doesn't cross over it probably is a waste of time and money to try and force it in a market where it doesn't belong. For instance, the people with the game about building houses may do well attending trade shows in the toy and building/construction industries but would likely do miserably at a book show.

More shows exist than are listed here. The reasons are simple. First, no one needs to or can attend every show which takes place. In fact, it's physically impossible for one person to even work every day at every show in just the gift industry. Only major shows in each industry are listed. Second, many shows are not long lived. If not established, they may draw large crowds for a year or two then, as attendance drops, vanish from the circuit.

Toy Shows—Trade

Trade shows for the toy industry are listed below. These shows generally are not open to the public and exhibit space must be booked a considerable time in advance. The name of the show is followed by the month in which it is held, the location, who to contact for more information (a phone number or address) and, occasionally, notes on the show.

International Toy Fair —January
Paris, France
(212) 869-1720

Harrogate International Toy Fair—January
North Yorkshire, England
Harrogate International Toy Fair Ltd.
8-9 Upper Street
Islington, London, UK N10PP

Hobby Industry of America Convention—January
Location varies
(201) 794-1133

Only certain types of games tend to do well at this show so get a copy of last year's attendance list and check to see the types of games being sold there.

Milan Toy Fair—January
Milan, Italy
E-A Salone
International Fair
Del Giocattolo via petit
Milan, Italy

British Toy and Hobby Fair—January
Earl's Court
80 Camberwell Road
London, England, UK SE5 0EG

Canadian Toy and Decoration Fair—January
Toronto, Canada
(416) 893-1689

Hong Kong Toys & Games Fair
Hong Kong Convention Center
(212) 838-8688

Winter Consumer Electronics Show
Las Vegas Convention Center
(202) 457-8700

Nuremberg Toy Fair—February
Nuremberg, Germany
International Speilwarenmesse
DgMBh 85
Nuremberg, West Germany

American Toy Fair—February
New York City
(212) 675-1141

This is the big one, at least for this country. Very important to have representation at both the permanent show rooms at the 200 Fifth Avenue Building and the temporary exhibitor's hall.

Game Manufacturers Association Trade Show—March
Moves from city to city
Contact: Howard Barasch (214) 247-7981

Small but important show. Less than 1,000 buyers attend but they are all game buyers. No other types of products are exhibited. Very focused and conducts excellent retail seminar programs.

Game Inventors of America Conference—March or April
Moves from city to city
Contact: Steve Peek (214) 331-4587

Not a trade show. This acclaimed, intensive two day conference features product acquisition heads from major game companies in fourteen seminars and eight workshops. Active G.I.A. members apply for private interview sessions. If you want to learn about the game business this is the single most important event to attend.

Midwest Toy & Hobby Show—March
Chicago, IL
(614) 452-4541

Dallas Toy Show—March
Dallas, TX
(214) 655-6100

Southeastern Toy Fair—March
Atlanta, GA
(404) 231-2320

Pacific Northwest Toy Show
Seattle International Trade Center
(206) 441-8442

Western States Toy and Hobby Show—April
Los Angeles, CA
(213) 380-2229

International Toy Fair—May
Tokyo, Japan
Japan International Toy Fair Association
11-14, 3-Chome
Kotobuki, Taito-Ku, Tokyo, JN

GENCON—August
Lake Geneva, WI
P.O. Box 756
Lake Geneva, WI 53147

This one is a consumer convention focusing on fantasy/role playing games but sometimes a good place to show new product to consumers. 1992 attendance was nearly 20,000 people.

Dallas Toy Show—September
Dallas, TX
(214) 655-6186

Southeastern Spring/Summer Toy Fair—September
Atlanta, GA
(404) 231-2320

New England Toy Rep Show—October
Stoughton, MA
(617) 449-2345

Spring & Summer Toy & Hobby Show—October
Los Angeles, CA
(213) 380-2229

Hong Kong Toy & Gift Fair—October
Hong Kong
(212) 730-0777

Taiwan Toy & Gift Fair—October
Taipei, Taiwan
(212) 532-7055

Toy Manufacturers of America—December
New York, NY
(212) 675-1141

Gift Shows—Trade   At last count there were 128 different gift shows conducted annually within the United States. If each show averaged three days in length there would be more show days in the year than there are days in the year. The major shows are listed below.

Atlanta National Gift Show—January
Atlanta Market Center
Atlanta, GA
(404) 688-8994

The Beckman Gift Show—January
L.A. Sports Arena
Los Angeles, CA
(213) 682-3661

L.A. Gift Mart—January
L.A. Mart
Los Angeles, CA
(213) 749-7911

Charlotte Mart—January
Charlotte Merchandise Mart
Charlotte, NC
(704) 377-5881

Dallas Gift Show—January
Dallas Market Center
Dallas, TX
(214) 655-6276

Chicago Mart Gift Show—January
Chicago Mart
Chicago, IL
(312) 527-4141

Chicago Gift Show—January
McCormick Place
Chicago, IL
(708) 310-1222

San Francisco Gift Show—February
Moscone Center
San Francisco, CA
(415) 621-7345

San Francisco Gift Center—February
S.F. Gift Center
San Francisco, CA
(415) 861-7733

New York Gift Show—February
Javits Center
New York, NY
(212) 686-6070

New York Merchandise Mart—February
New York, NY
(212) 686-1203

New York Gift Building—February
225 Fifth Avenue
New York, NY
(212) 685-6377

National Stationery Show—May
Javits Center
New York, NY
(212) 686-6070

Dallas Gift Show—July
Dallas Market Center
Dallas, TX
(214) 655-6276

Atlanta National Gift Show—July
Atlanta Market Center
Atlanta, GA
(404) 688-8994

The Beckman Gift Show—July
L.A. Sports Arena
Los Angeles, CA
(213) 665-5713

L.A. Mart—July
L.A. Mart
Los Angeles, CA
(213) 749-7911

California Gift Show—July
Convention Center
Los Angeles, CA
(213) 682-3661

Chicago Mart Gift Show—July
Chicago Mart
Chicago, IL
(312) 527-4141

Chicago Gift Show—July
McCormick Place
Chicago, IL
(708) 310-1222

San Francisco Gift Show—August
Moscone Center
San Francisco, CA
(415) 621-7345

San Francisco Gift Center—August
S.F. Gift Center
San Francisco, CA
(415) 861-7733

New York Gift Show—August
Javits Center
New York, NY
(212) 686-6070

New York Merchandise Mart—August
New York, NY
(212) 686-1203

New York Gift Building—August
225 Fifth Avenue
New York, NY
(212) 685-6377

Educational Shows   Each state has one or more conventions for its educators, teachers, administrators, and directors. Most of these shows are open to vendors to rent exhibit space. If a game has genuine inherent educational value these shows may prove to be most effective. There are two major national shows listed below. To find out about individual state shows contact the appropriate state agency.

National Education Association Convention—June or July
Moves from city to city
(202) 833-4000

Educational Dealers & Supply Association Show—March or April
Moves from city to city
(315) 789-0458

Book Shows   There are a number of regional small book shows. The two listed below are the largest. To obtain information on others contact either or both of the associations below.

American Booksellers Association Book Show—April or May
Moves from city to city
(212) 867-9060

American Library Association Convention—May or June
Moves from city to city
(312) 944-6780

TRADE ASSOCIATIONS

The following is a list of associations which are related to the gaming industry. It is not always necessary to join the organizations to obtain help in getting information as most exist to promote their particular industry.

Game Inventors of America
P.O. Box 58711
World Trade Center
Dallas, TX 75258
(214) 331-4587

Game Manufacturers Association
803 Fourth Avenue
Grinnell, IA 50112
(515) 236-5027

Canadian Toy Manufacturers Association
P.O. Box 294
Kleinburg, Ontario
Canada L0J 1C0
(416) 893-1689

Electronic Industries Association Consumer Electronic Group
2001 Eye Street
Washington, DC 20006
(202) 457-4919

Hobby Industries Of America
319 East 54th Street
Elmwood, NJ 07407
(201) 794-1133

Juvenile Products Manufacturers Association
66 East Main Street
Moorestown, NJ 08057
(609) 234-9155

Midwest Toy & Hobby Association
100 East Ogden Avenue
Westmont, IL 60559
(312) 850-7977

Southwestern Toy & Hobby Association
World Trade Center #58310
Dallas, TX 75258
(214) 742-2448

Toy Manufacturers of America
200 Fifth Avenue, Suite 740
New York, NY 10010
(212) 675-1141

Toy Wholesalers' Association of America
66 E. Main Street
Moorestown, NJ 08067
(609) 234-9155

American Booksellers Association
560 White Plains Road
Tarrytown, NY 10591
(914) 631-7800

American Library Association
50 East Huron Street
Chicago, IL 60611
(312) 944-6780

Educational Dealers and Suppliers Association
P.O. Box 1080
Geneva, NY 14456
(315) 789-0458

GLOSSARY OF PRINTING TERMS

ART DIRECTOR—Individual in charge of one or more artists who directs their efforts.

ARTWORK—An image prepared for graphic reproduction.

BANDING—The wrapping of a package with string, rubber bands, etc., to secure the contents as a single unit.

BASIS WEIGHT—The weight of 500 sheets of a particular size and class of paper.

BLUELINE—A photographic proof consisting of blue images on white background.

BOOK—Any published work of more than 64 pages.

BOOKLET—Any published work of 64 pages or less.

BREAKING FOR COLOR—Dividing artwork into specific color overlays, or forms, during the artwork stages.

BROWNLINE—A photographic proof consisting of brown images on white background.

BUYOUTS—Services purchased from an outside source.

C1S—Paper stock which is coated on one side.

C2S—Paper stock which is coated on both sides.

CALIPER—see paper caliper.

CAMERA-READY ART—Graphic artwork which is ready for photographic reproduction.

CLIP ART—Preprinted art images sold to printers to be cut out and applied directly to artwork.

COATED PAPERS—Paper made with a fine coat of mineral substance to enhance its printability.

COLLATING—The gathering of several different items into one organized group.

COLOR SEPARATION—Photographic process by which a color image is divided into the three primary colors and black film images using filters.

COMPOSITION—The typesetting of copy in a selected size and style of type.

COMPREHENSIVE—A completed visualization of an image prepared by an artist; final step before preparation of finished art. Sometimes called a comp.

CUTTING—The separation of larger sheets of paper into smaller ones.

DRILLING—The operation of creating round holes in paper or other materials.

DUMMY—A folded sample representing a book, booklet, or image to be reproduced; used for planning.

ENLARGER—A piece of photographic equipment which enlarges images.

FILLER WORK—Printing jobs taken into the plant, usually at a lower billing rate, to smooth out peaks and valleys of the production schedule.

FLAT—Assemblage of film and masking base materials during the image assembly (stripping) phases.

FLAT COLOR—Colors which are specifically mixed to match a sample.

FONT — A complete assortment of all characters in one size and series of type.

FORM—A collection of images on one plate which will be printed in the same color. Also called a printer.

FREELANCE ARTIST — A self-employed person who produces graphic art.

GATHERING—see collating.

GRAIN DIRECTION—The alignment of fibers in a sheet of paper. Long grain being the length and Short grain being the width of a sheet of paper.

HALFTONE—Reproduction of an image by a pattern of dots of varying sizes and shapes, as related to the light or dark areas of the image.

IMAGE ASSEMBLY — Procedure by which film images are positioned in a precise order for platemaking. Also called stripping.

INK COVERAGE — Percentage factor related to the density of ink and the area covered.

JOGGING—The alignment of paper into very even piles to facilitate production.

LABOR INTENSIVE—Term describing a condition which requires large numbers of man hours to be spent to obtain a desired result.

LEADING—The amount of white space between lines of type.

LIFT—A hand held stack of paper to be worked.

LINE COPY—Material prepared for reproduction consisting only of high contrast images, lines or dots.

"M"—One thousand.

MECHANICAL—Artwork which has been fully prepared for reproduction as the first step of a print job.

MOIRE — An undesirable pattern formed when two or more dotted screen areas are incorrectly overlapped.

NEGATIVE—An image on film or paper where the image is clear or white and the background is black.

NUMBERING OPERATION — Wherein consecutive numbers are printed.

OPAQUE — Liquid product painted on film with a brush to cover imperfections.

OVERLAY—Transparent sheets used to separate colors mechanically on art work. Usually one overlay per color.

PADDING — Application of adhesive for temporary binding of paper in pads.

PALLET—see Skid.

PAPER CALIPER—The thickness of paper stock measured in thousandths of inches (or points).

PASTE-UP—see Mechanical.

PERFORATED—Small dash cuts made in paper to facilitate tearing.

PICA — A common unit of measurement in typesetting and copy preparation. One pica equals twelve points and there are approximately 6 picas to an inch.

PLY—Term used to indicate thickness of cardboard. To convert to caliper, multiply the ply value by 3 then add 6 to the results.

PMT — A product manufactured by Kodak and used to go directly from camera to paste-up.

POINT (paper)—The equivalent of one thousandth of an inch.

POINT (printer's)—Basis for typesetting, where one point equals $1/72$ of an inch.

PRESS-ON TYPE — Letters which are transferred from a master sheet to artwork by pressing or rubbing. Also called rub-on or transfer type.

PRESS PREPARATION or MAKEREADY—The segment of press operation which sets the press up for a particular job to be printed.

PRESS RUNNING — The continuous operation of a press during which acceptable sheets are being printed for a particular job.

PRINTING TRADE CUSTOMS—The operations and business practices held as legal based upon court precedent; usually printed on the reverse side of quotations or proposals.

PROCESS COLORS—Specially formulated pigments used in printing process color separations; magenta (red-blue), cyan (blue-green), yellow (red-green) and black as transparent colors. Often called process red, process blue, process yellow and process black.

PROOFING—The visual checking of a job in production.

REGISTRATION MARKS—Usually appear as two lines in crossed form centered in a circle. Used throughout printing production to align (register) images.

SADDLE STITCHING—The use of wire or other material along the spine (saddle) of gathered signatures, holding them together. Usually one or more staples.

SCORED—The creasing of paper stock to provide a line for folding.

SCREEN TINTS—Pieces of film used to divide normally solid areas into design or patterns; two major categories include dots and special effects.

SCRIBING—The manual removal of film emulsion using a scribing tool or knife. Usually only done to make simple corrections of film images.

SIGNATURE — A collection of printed pages on a master sheet, folded in a prearranged sequence to make all or part of a book or booklet.

SKID — Wooden or metal base with runners upon which paper is stacked in large quantities.

STEP AND REPEAT — Procedure by which a single film image is reproduced in a defined manner to provide multiple exact images.

STRIPPER — Individual who mounts film images into flats to complete image assembly.

STRIPPING — See Image Assembly.

THUMBNAIL — Sketches produced by an artist during the initial stages of artwork for a graphic image.

TRIMMING — The removal of edges or segments of paper stock to bring the final printed product to the desired size.

UNCOATED PAPER — Paper which does not receive a chemical coating.

UNIT COST — Cost for an individual item or product.

UP — The number of finished sized sheets which can be positioned and printed on a single press run.

WASHUP — The procedure used for removing ink from a press.

ABOUT THE AUTHOR

Steve Peek is a twenty year industry veteran who has placed his mark on nearly two hundred published games. His understanding of the industry is broad and deep. Steve's activities have run the gamut; from helping dozens of entrepreneurial start-ups to manufacturing components for such blockbusters as *PICTIONARY* and licensing games to television shows and movies. There are few outside major game companies who can match the breadth of his knowledge and expertise in the game industry. His willingness to share this inside information prompted noted psychotherapist Jamie Turndorf, inventor of the new game *LOVE QUEST*, to describe him as "the Encyclopedia Britannica of games."

Peek founded GAME INVENTORS OF AMERICA (G.I.A.), a member funded society, to provide an information and resource center. G.I.A. provides newsletters, updates, educational conferences, and cooperative sales programs to help inventors find success in the game industry.

Since 1979 Steve has been employed by Dallas-based Yaquinto Printing Company, one of the world's leading contract manufacturers of games and cards, where he is director of publications as well as offering consulting services. In addition to being president of G.I.A. he sits on the board of directors for the GAME MANUFACTURERS ASSOCIATION, is a principal of GAMEPLAN, a development agency which evaluates games and represents game inventors, and serves on various industry panels.

His marketing experience extends to toy, book, educational, gift and traditional game markets. He has been a keynote speaker at conventions, universities, meetings, and trade shows.

For additional information about invention evaluations and representation, please write: Steve Peek, Box 58780 World Trade Center, Dallas, TX 75258.

Index

A complete catalog of Betterway Books is available FREE by writing to the address shown below, or by calling toll-free 1-800-289-0963. To order additional copies of this book, send in retail price of the book plus, $3.00 postage and handling for one book, and $1.00 for each additional book. Ohio residents add 5½% sales tax. Allow 30 days for delivery.

Betterway Books
1507 Dana Avenue
Cincinnati, Ohio 45207

Stock is limited on some titles; prices subject to change without notice.